Endorsements

"This guide was one of the most informative books I've read. I started reading it in the morning and couldn't put it down until I finished it. I kept finding more information of value that I did not know about, and I've been reading books for more than ninety years."

Dick Savage, Columnist, *Notre Dame Magazine*

"Wow, a great and much-needed book. I am 62 and don't feel old and am using the resources outlined in *Invent Your Retirement* as a cerebral 'Ponce de Leon.' It works! I have always felt that if I do what I like, I will never work a day in my life. The advice and wisdom contained in this guide will keep me forever young."

Brooks Mitchell, Ph.D., Associate Professor of Management and Marketing, University of Wyoming, and President, Snowfly.com

"Art Koff's *Invent Your Retirement* is a must-read for anyone contemplating this journey. His advice—from weaving your way through Social Security, becoming computer savvy, and even stopping smoking and everything in between—makes retiring so much less stressful. I know because I used it, and it saved countless hours of searching for this information."

Carol Kleiman, Author and Nationally Syndicated Columnist, retired

"*Invent Your Retirement* is just the kind of reference guide that our senior readers need. It provides content on every subject of interest as well as referencing where they can go to find more information. An absolute must-read not only for seniors, but also for younger people responsible for the well-being of senior family members."

Jim Moss, Publisher, *The Times Herald-Record*, Middletown, NY

"An excellent resource about activities, finances, and health. Keep it on your desk for ready reference."

Dr. Nancy K. Schlossberg, Ed.D., Professor Emerita at the University of Maryland, and author, speaker, and recognized expert on mid-life, aging, transitions, and coping

"'Knowledge is power.' Art Koff has combined his experience, insights, and research to give people entering the 'third age' of their lives the power to succeed in creating a fulfilling retirement. This resource covers all the bases and then gives the reader more—with checklists, tips and lists to motivate and inspire."

Lori Bitter, Partner, JWT Mature Market Group

"Every senior and everyone advising seniors should own this book. It is an essential resource for those in or preparing for retirement."

Dan Berman, CPCU, CLU, JD, Insurance Agent/Advisor, The Rockwood Company

"After reading Art's book, I can't imagine there is a more useful and practical resource for seniors. It is well researched, timely, and easy to read. As an accountant, I found the topics he covered to be of paramount importance to those close to or in retirement. Unfortunately many of these areas are ignored until it's too late."

Jeffrey Arnol, CPA, JD, Managing Partner, Kessler Orlean Silver & Co., Certified Public Accountants

"Filled with solid information and insights, Koff's book is a terrific resource for retirees and those contemplating retirement."

Joyce Gioia, CMC, CSP, Strategic Business Futurist and Author

"Being a boomer myself, I found Koff's new book very timely. At last people understand that the demographic changes in this country will only worsen the talent wars, and *Invent Your Retirement* comprehensively addresses this issue. The book is a must-read."

Tim Gibbon, President & CEO, JWT Specialized Communications, New York

"As a former publisher I found this book not only full of valuable information for seniors, but loaded with reference materials for those of us who wanted or needed more in-depth information. Every senior should have a copy in their library."

James Gerard, Publisher (retired), Ashgate Publishing, and Vice President (retired), XEROX Educational Publishing

"Informative, valuable, easy to navigate, and written to be understood by all. That is a rare combination and represents just a few of the many attributes in this reference guide. Art Koff is to be applauded for his wisdom and insight into the needs of those preparing for or already in retirement. *Invent Your Retirement* is not only a must-read, it needs to be close by at all times. Bravo!"

Marvin Goldsmith, President (retired), Campbell Mithun Advertising Agency

"Art Koff has been a leader and innovator for over thirty years. His unique insights into the future are a must-read for anyone contemplating retirement. I strongly endorse *Invent Your Retirement* for people of all ages."

Joseph G. Shaker, President, Shaker Recruitment & Advertising Services

INVENT YOUR RETIREMENT

Resources for the Good Life

ART KOFF

OAKHILL PRESS
Winchester, Virginia

Copyright 2006 Art Koff

All rights reserved.

Reproduction or translation of any part of this work beyond that permitted by Section 107 or 108 of the 1976 United States Copyright Act without the permission of the copyright owner is unlawful. Requests for permission or further information should be addressed to the Permissions Department, Oakhill Press.

This publication is designed to provide accurate and authoritative information in regard to the subject matter covered. It is sold with the understanding that the publisher is not engaged in rendering legal, accounting, or other professional service. If legal advice or other expert assistance is required, the services of a competent professional person should be sought. *From a Declaration of Principles jointly adopted by a committee of the American Bar Association and a committee of publishers.*

Without limiting the rights under copyright reserved above, no part of this publication may be reproduced, stored in or introduced into a retrieval system, or transmitted, in any form or by any means (electronic, mechanical, photocopying, recording or otherwise) without the prior written permission of the publisher of this book.

10 9 8 7 6 5 4 3 2 1

Cover design: Janice B. Benight
Text design: Craig Hines
Cover photo: David Toase/Getty Images

Library of Congress Cataloging in Publication Data

Koff, Art, 1935–
　　Invent your retirement : resources for the good life / compiled by Art Koff.
　　　p.　cm.
　　ISBN 1-886939-76-4
　　1. Retirement — United States — Planning.　2. Retirement, Places of — United States.　I. Title.
　　HQ1063.2.U6K65　　2006
　　646.7'90973—dc22　　　　　　　　　　　　　　　　　　　　　　2005031800

Oakhill Press
1647 Cedar Grove Road
Winchester, VA 22603
800-32-books
Printed in the United States of America

Contents

Preface . . . . ***v***
Acknowledgment . . . . ***vii***

Chapter 1
Retired Brains Need Exercise *1*

Chapter 2
Where Do Retirees Live? *19*

Chapter 3
Start Your Home Office *25*

Chapter 4
Volunteering *31*

Chapter 5
Continue Your Education *37*

Chapter 6
Become Computer Literate *53*

Chapter 7
Protect Your Good Credit *85*

Chapter 8
Health Insurance Costs *89*

Chapter 9
Prescription Drugs *93*

Chapter 10
Assisted Living and Long Term Care Insurance *115*

Chapter 11
Live Better and Longer *121*

Chapter 12
Memory Loss *133*

Chapter 13
Get a Pet *141*

Chapter 14
Funding Your Retirement *151*

Chapter 15
Estate Planning *177*

Chapter 16
When Friends Pass On *191*

Appendices *197*

About the Author *222*

Preface

This is a book for seniors, those of us who are retired or are approaching retirement. A number of my friends have asked me for help in finding reference material to help them locate information in a wide variety of areas. Much of this material is readily available, but as far as I know there is no single place that contains a good deal of it. When you are a senior you don't like to spend time searching for anything, so I decided to put together a list of "Resources for the Good Life" as a helpful guide for us "Retired Brains."

In doing so I have regularly used the research that others have assembled. I have attempted to give proper credit even when I have rewritten, shortened, and substantially edited the materials. I have also provided contact information for those of you who wish to get more in-depth information. Sometimes I've included phone numbers, sometimes books and articles, but most often I've provided URLs or Internet destinations. For those of you who are not able to use a computer to reach the Internet, I'm sorry. For some of the more important information I hope you will ask a friend, your children, or your grandchildren to use their computer to reach this information for you. I have included source information to make this search easier.

Seniors who have not as yet taken the Internet plunge, I urge you to do so. It is a great deal easier to learn how to use the Internet than most people think. You do not need any special technical skills, although some typing ability helps. This book contains an easy-to-follow, step-by-step primer on how to use a computer to reach the Internet and particularly how to use e-mail.

I was lucky to be introduced to a computer when I was a "pre-senior" of 50. My mother decided I should become computer literate and against all of my protests bought me a computer. When I told her I was not interested in taking the time to learn how to use a computer, she told me to put it in my closet for whenever I did feel up to learning. Because it was there, I thought I may as well try and get on with it. It was a mother's challenge.

Invent Your Retirement: Resources for the Good Life is exactly what the forthcoming pages are all about. If you are already retired, you'll understand. If you are looking forward to retiring, you really have to join us to understand, and hopefully what you read here will help.

Note to the Reader

> Internet addresses, domain names, and URLs may change from time to time. If an Internet address or domain name in this book is not a working URL, it is suggested that the reader go to an Internet search engine and search for a current URL using the information provided. The author would very much appreciate your passing on any new URL found. Please e-mail him at artkoff@yahoo.com, providing the page number, new URL, and the URL being replaced. This information will help keep the resources in the book up to date for future editions.

Acknowledgments

In compiling this information I owe thanks to so many people I don't have room to include them all. At the governmental level I spoke with people at the Departments of Agriculture, Labor, State and the FDA, Social Security Administration and Medicare; who all went out of their way to provide me with access to information.

Special thanks must also be given to Alzheimer's Association and AARP not only for giving me permission to use material, but also for helping me find it.

Thanks also to Marcia Bench at CareerCoach, Valerie VanBooven, RN, BSN, PGCM, author of *Aging Answers*, Jeri Sedlar & Rick Miners authors of *Don't Retire, Rewire,* and Joel Mitchell for his help putting together the Home Office and Personal Information Guide.

And thanks to my neighbor and great cook, Dave Thomas, for his secret (not secret anymore) blueberry pie recipe.

Retired Brains Need Exercise

Chapter Overview

- Exercise Your Brain
- Redefining Retirement
- When Does Someone Become an "Older" Worker?
- How Demographics Help
- Work and Live Longer
- Why Seniors Work
- What Do Employers Want?
- Find a Part-time or Temporary Job
- Practical Steps to Help You Find a Job
- Firms That Will Help You Write Your Résumé
- Part-time & Temporary Jobs Often Filled by Seniors
- AARP's Best Employers for Workers Over 50: 2004 Honorees

So you're retired. You've thought about relaxing, enjoying yourself, traveling, doing all the things that for years you just did not have the time to do.

Exercise Your Brain

But you're bored. Every day for years you got up early and went to work. Now you still wake up early, but have no place to go. The alarm doesn't ring, but you're up anyway. All those pet projects are not enough to keep you busy, and fishing, golfing, and working around the house or yard are just not enough for you. And besides, your Social Security check coupled with other retirement income is not as much as you thought it would be. It does not cover your needs, let alone all the things you had hoped to do. That trip you wanted to take would eat into your savings.

Redefining Retirement

There is a solution for this dilemma. Take a job, even a part-time job. Many employers have found that hiring seniors like you is a cost-effective way to increase productivity. Employers hire seniors for some very challenging part-time and temporary assignments; often you can use the experience and expertise you've gained prior to retiring. You'd be surprised to know that according to *American Demographics* magazine's analysis of Bureau of Labor Statistics data, labor force participation for ages 55 to 64 is higher than you might expect. In 2002 it was 69 percent for men and 55 percent for women. It is projected that by 2012 it will be 75 percent for men and 64 percent for women. This means that three-quarters of male seniors and almost two-thirds of female seniors will still be working.

There is a new research study from the Heldrich Center for Workforce Development authored by Carl E. Van Horn, Ph.D., Kenneth Dautrich, and Samuel J. Best, Ph.D. This study can be accessed online by going to *http://www.heldrich.rutgers.edu/Resources/Publication/191/WT16.pdf*. For those of you who are not computer literate, I have copied, with permission, some of the information contained in this remarkable study. There is not room to include the entire survey, so I have chosen areas of particular interest. I have had to skip around a bit to include as much information as possible. I urge you to check out this valuable information and read the entire survey. If you need to, get someone who is Net literate to access it for you.

> As America's influential baby boom generation approaches retirement age, the vision of a traditional work-free retirement is yielding to a new notion of a work-filled retirement. While more than a quarter of American workers still expect their 60s and 70s to be devoted to leisure or community service, the majority of workers say that full- or part-time work will be either necessary or desirable. This new vision of how to spend time in one's later years will affect not only older workers but workers at all stages of their careers and employers across the nation.
>
> A work-filled retirement finds workers open to continued opportunities for meaningful work during their retirement years, with an undercurrent of anxiety over future income and benefits. They are less confident about being able to retire when they want than they were five years ago. Many suspect that employers favor younger workers over older workers, especially when layoffs occur. These employees also display surprisingly high levels of confidence that they will have adequate funds to support themselves during retirement.

The traditional notion of retirement, where one stops working completely and enjoys leisure time with friends and family—is obsolete. This national survey finds that about two-thirds of workers view retirement from a full-time job as an opportunity for continued productive employment. Nearly seven in ten workers expect to continue to work full-time or part-time following retirement from their main job, including 15 percent who expect to start their own business. Only 13 percent expect to stop working entirely.

Interest in a work-filled life for older workers increased significantly after the stock market declined in 2001. In spring 2005, nearly a quarter of the American workers surveyed report that they would be working either full-time or part-time for needed income following retirement, compared with only 13 percent in fall 2000. Older workers are one of the fastest-growing components of the U.S. workforce. The Bureau of Labor Statistics estimates that between 2002 and 2012, the number of workers 55 years and older is expected to grow by nearly 50 percent, far outpacing increases in the number of

Figure 1.1
Retirement Percentage by Age Group

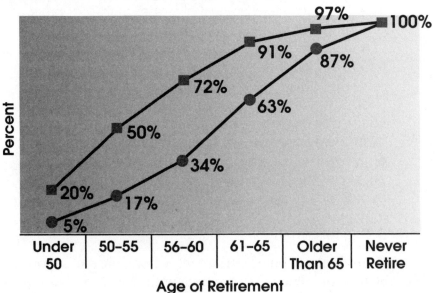

workers aged 16 to 54. By 2012, workers 55 years and older will make up about 20 percent of the labor force.

In fact, among today's workers who are retired but still in the workforce, 54 percent went back to work because they needed income. Between 2000 and 2005, there was also a drop in the number of workers who said they would work part-time out of interest or enjoyment.

The survey finds deepening concern among workers about their ability to retire when they want. Although half of workers would like to retire by age 55, only 17 percent believe they will be able to do so. Additionally, the gap between when workers would like to retire and when they think they will able to retire has widened since 2000.

Six in 10 respondents now believe they will not be able to retire from full-time work by age 60, including 12 percent who say they will never be able to retire. In contrast, in 2000, only 40 percent of workers surveyed doubted they could retire by age 60, with 7 percent saying they would never be able to retire.

When Does Someone Become an "Older" Worker?

A majority of workers do not consider themselves to qualify as "older workers" until at least the age of 60, while maintaining that employers classify them as old at much earlier ages. There is a large gap between workers' self-assessments of their relative age and the way they believe employers view them.

A work-filled retirement emerges with the United States in the midst of a demographic transformation. The oldest of the baby-boom generation will start to turn 65—the traditional retirement age—in 2011, and the youngest of that generation will turn 55 in 2019. In coming years, older workers will have a growing presence in the U.S. workforce. By 2012, workers 40 years and older will make up over half of the labor force.

As baby boomers near retirement, a new vision for retirement is taking hold among American workers. A majority of workers look forward to a productive retirement focused on working out of interest or for enjoyment, supplementing their incomes, or starting new businesses that contribute to the economy. Others expect to remain active through volunteer activities.

At a time when the number of workers 55 years and older is growing rapidly, this survey finds widespread skepticism about the treatment of older employees in the workplace. Older workers are perceived to be likely targets of layoffs and are likely to face a hard landing following job loss. In light of these beliefs, a majority of workers believe that both employers and government have a responsibility to promote employment opportunities for older workers.

In evaluating the traditional three pillars of retirement security—employer-sponsored pension plans, government benefits, and personal savings—workers express a combination of confidence and concern. Those surveyed are optimistic about the ability of employer-sponsored pensions and retirement plans to generate promised benefits, despite a spate of recent reports about the funding challenges facing many private-sector plans. Workers reveal more anxiety when asked about the other two pillars of retirement security. Although personal savings are the second most commonly cited source of primary retirement income—after employer-sponsored pension plans—more than a third of workers are currently saving nothing besides Social Security, and less than half think they are doing a good job of saving for retirement. When asked about government retirement programs, large numbers of workers express skepticism about the future availability of Social Security and Medicare, as they did in 2000. Only about one in five workers strongly believes that both will be available to support them in retirement.

How Demographics Help
The demographic shifts in the U.S. workforce are likely to increase pressure on the nation's political and corporate leaders to come up with creative policy solutions. The imminent retirement of the oldest baby boomers will put increasing strains on government retirement programs and the economy. At the same time, the growing presence of older workers in the labor force is likely to force changes in employers' policies and workplace practices. Policymakers should look for solutions that facilitate a work-filled retirement for employees that choose it, meet the needs of employers for a steady supply of qualified workers, and address the need of all workers for retirement security.

Work and Live Longer
An Israeli study of one thousand people who continued to work at the age of 70 and beyond found that this group was 2.5 times as likely to be alive at the age of 82 than those who had retired and weren't working at the beginning of the study. The study results seemed to indicate that the longer you keep working, the better.

According to an article in the *Wall Street Journal,* "Research has shown that remaining challenged, especially cognitively challenged, can provide a boost to longevity." The article goes on to quote Dr. Michael DeBakey, who at 96 said, "Work can block out the unpleasant things we have to deal with every day. When you concentrate, you are not distracted by the things that are bothering you."

Why Seniors Work
If you are not interested in working because you are bored, you might very well be grappling with one of the four horsemen of retirement security: your pension (via a company or your own IRA or retirement plan), Social Security, personal

savings/net worth, and health insurance. A shortfall in any of these requires some additional income after you reach what you thought would be your retirement age.

IMPORTANT NOTE: The cost of Medicare premiums is rising much faster than is generally known to the average senior. With skyrocketing medical costs the increase in 2005 is 17.5 percent. It is projected that without substantial Medicare reform the Medicare cost for a typical retiree in 2040 who receives $1,335 a month from Social Security will be $292 monthly.

To give you a better idea of what this is all about, look at Figure 1.2.

You will see that in the coming years employers must focus more on employing seniors if they are to find enough workers. With such a large percentage of workers in the 55+ age group, employers are already developing plans to better utilize seniors in the workplace. (See more charts in the appendix.) Numbers in the chart represent the percentage change in the population in these age groups 1995–2000 vs. 2000–2010.

Figure 1.2

Change in the U.S. Older Population, by Age Group:

Selected Time Periods, 1995–2010*

Time Period	Under 60	50+	55+	60+	65+	75+	85+	100+
1995–2000	4.6	11.1	7.3	4.1	3.5	12.1	17.2	33.3
2000–2010	5.6	27.0	27.3	22.6	13.5	10.7	33.2	81.9

*Source: U.S. Bureau of the Census, Current Population Reports, P25–1130, "Population Projections of the United States, by Age."

A recent Merrill Lynch retirement survey of more than three thousand boomers reported that 83 percent intend to keep working, and 56 percent of them hope to do so in a new profession. According to AARP, eight out of ten baby boomers say they plan to work in retirement. The numbers break down as follows per the AARP survey.

Plan to work part-time for interest or enjoyment . . . . . . 30 percent
Plan to work part-time for income . . . . 25 percent
Plan to start their own business. . . . . 15 percent
Plan to work full-time in a new job or career . . . . 7 percent
Have other reasons to continue working . . . . 3 percent

A *Wall Street Journal* report indicated that 68 percent of current workers expect to work for pay in some capacity after they retire. So why shouldn't you join the majority of the people in your age group?

Some seniors don't feel that employers are interested in hiring them. Some have had a bad experience and, after all, if employers are offering early retirement, why would they want to hire those same seniors they have pushed out the door?

What Do Employers Want?

Actually, employers are interested in hiring you, as they have found that seniors provide:

- Quality customer service experience
- Stability
- Ability to initiate sales and transaction dependability
- Eagerness to provide support and guidance
- Superior communication skills
- Varied work experience
- Better ability to work with mature clientele
- An old-fashioned work ethic*

*From Helen Foster, Mature Market Group, *Tapping the Mature Workforce: An Overview & Recommendations*

Many employers have found that hiring older workers provides them with employees who are more likely to be punctual, are more committed to quality, have better people skills, are less likely to be absent from work, are not job changers, possess excellent customer service skills, require less training, and generally have a more positive attitude. In almost every area other than their knowledge of technology, older workers provide employers with a more cost-effective hire than do their younger counterparts.

Employers have also found that hiring seniors for project assignments or on a part-time basis can save them big-time dollars on benefits and health-care costs, as in most cases seniors do not expect benefits. Of course, many seniors continue working full-time for the money, and an increasingly larger percentage continue working in order to receive health-care coverage for themselves and their family

The majority of small-business owners asked indicate that health-care benefits coverage is their biggest challenge due to increasing costs. Often the same is true for large corporations. Hiring seniors to work part-time or on temporary assignments in most cases saves these health-care benefits costs.

Find a Part-time or Temporary Job

Jeri Sedlar and Rick Miners, coauthors of *Don't Retire, Rewire*, suggest answering the following questions to get you thinking.

1. Why do I want to find new work or pursue my dream job?
2. If it's for financial reasons, is it to replace, supplement, or continue to build up wealth?
3. How do I want to work: part-time, full-time, seasonally, on-call, or project-by-project?
4. Where would I like to work: a corporation, on the beach, home office, or retail store?
5. With whom do I want to work: alone, with my spouse or partner, prior coworkers, children, the elderly?

6. What current interests/themes/patterns do I have?
7. Which ones could lead me into a new career?
8. What things would I like to work with: animals, flowers, art, food, photography, cars?
9. What do/did I like/love in my current/most recent past work?
10. What do/did I dislike or even hate doing for work and why?
11. What accomplishments am I most proud of? Why?
12. What beyond money drives or motivates me to work?
13. What do I really value in my life that could affect my work-direction decision?
14. What skills/strengths do I want to use? What new ones do I want to get?
15. What are my "must-haves" from my next work engagement?
16. What was the best job I ever had? Why?
17. Am I willing to go back to school or be an apprentice if my dream job called for it?

Practical Steps to Help You Find a Job

So going back to work part-time sounds pretty good, and it looks like employers could use your experience. Where should you look? What do you need to do?

Register with temp agencies. Most of these agencies are not interested in your age, but rather whether you have the skills and experience to do the job their client has listed with them. If you are able to work unusual hours, times that most people are not interested in working, make sure to tell the temp counselor as well as list this on your application. Some temp agencies will even provide training if you lack appropriate skills, and of course there is always a bit of on-the-job training once you start working as each employer needs to educate you as to their specific needs. Working through a temporary agency also builds your résumé and can help you find temporary or part-time work more easily.

There are a host of Web sites to assist seniors in finding work. There is no cost to you to search for a job on these sites or to post your résumé. Some of the sites have listings of jobs from employers, and others provide you with information to help you in your job search.

http://www.retiredbrains.com/
   (best free job search site)
http://www.seniors4hire.org/
   (good career site)
http://www.retireecareers.com/
   (good career research site)
http://www.yourencore.com/
   (research/technical jobs only)
http://www.seniorjobbank.org/links/
   (important links for seniors)
http://www.jobsforretirees.com/
   (subsidiary of Executive Search Online)
http://www.seniorjobbank.org/
   (lots of résumés)
http://www.grayhairmanagement.com/
   (executives and managers)
http://www.seniorhelpwanted.com/
http://www.seniorsjobs.com/
http://www.experienceworks.org/
http://www.theretiredworker.com
http://www.ncoa.org/
   (National Council on Aging)
http://www.edd.ca.gov/eddswtx.htm
   (State of California)

Here's how this site works.
1. Start at main page: *http://www.ca.gov*
2. Select: Labor and Employment
3. Select: Targeted Services for Older Workers and Women
4. Reach numerous site links

http://www.doleta.gov/seniors/
   (U.S. Department of Labor Senior Community Service Employment Program)
http://www.score.org/
   (America's small business assistance)
http://www.thasc.com/
   (South Florida for-profit site hires seniors and the disabled)
http://www.seniorsforjobs.com/
   (Canadian)
http://www.maturityworks.com/content/index.asp
   (U.K. site)

If you are looking for a full-time job, the following major job boards have the most listings. All offer you the opportunity to post your résumé at no charge, but the jobs posted are not specifically designed for seniors.

http://www.monster.com/
http://www.careerbuilder.com/
http://hotjobs.yahoo.com/
http://4jobs.com/
http://beyond.com/

Depending on your skills and education you may need to revise your résumé (assuming you had one in the first place). The résumé you used when you last searched for a full-time job is no longer appropriate. Don't try and rewrite it yourself. Go to a professional. Costs vary, but should average about $250. This expenditure is a good investment for your future work.

Firms That Will Help You Write Your Résumé

Firms that will rewrite your résumé or give you tips on writing your résumé include:

http://www.free-resume-tips.com/ Phone 425-398-7378
http://www.1-on-1-resumes.com/ Phone 1-800-717-7094
http://www.resumeedge.com/ Phone 1-888-GET AN EDGE

For a directory of career coaches and résumé writers, some of whom specialize in working with retirees, go to *www.careercoachinstitute.com*.

Part-time and Temporary Jobs Often Filled by Seniors

Following is a list of jobs, not presented in any kind of order, often filled by seniors:

- Retail sales clerk
- Call center/customer service
- Cashier
- Greeter
- White-collar clerical or office support, reception, administrative assistant
- Professional (specialty or related specialty prior to retiring)
- Skilled or semi-skilled labor (specialty or related specialty prior to retiring)
- Inside sales (telemarketing)
- Real estate sales
- Outside sales
- Guard or security work
- Owning a small store
- Starting a business
- Consulting
- Franchisee
- Working in a family business
- Teaching
- Health services
- Farming
- Craft work
- Home improvement/repair
- Artist
- Cleaning (housekeeping, custodian, janitorial)
- Bookkeeping
- Truck driver
- Manager/assistant manager/supervisor

Consider working or consulting part-time for your old company. Your ex-employer might be interested in your taking on an assignment or project for a week or two, or even a month or two. Temporary assignments are a win/win situation for both you and an employer.

If you are interested in checking out salary information in your field or line of work as well as the region of the country in which you live, look at the Salary Wizard at *http://www.Salary.com*. You can also check Salary Information links at Job Star (*http://www.jobsmart.org*) and *http://www.Salaries Review.com*. Some of the information at Salary.com is not free, and there is a small charge for all of the information at *http://salariesreview.com/*.

Some retirees wish to work in a field where they have had experience, while others are looking for something quite different from what they have done most of their lives. Don't be limited by these lists. Look for something you've always wanted—particularly if what you earn is not as important to you as what you do.

The job market has changed radically even in the past ten years. Online portfolios, Web logs (blogs), and customized narrative bios are just a few of the tools being used by job seekers today. Using them can show that you are current in the use of technology and help overcome any hint of age bias too!

When seeking part-time or full-time work, either in retirement or late career, keep in mind the following information from Marcia Bench, a Master Certified Career Coach. Marcia has nineteen years' experience in career development and is the founder and director of Career Coach Institute, LLC, and Retirement Coach Institute. A frequent speaker and the author of eighteen books including *Career Coaching: An Insider's Guide* and *Retire Your Way,* Marcia suggests the following:

- **Take the time to clarify your career goal.** "If you don't know where you're going, any road will take you there." What would you *love* to do (even if you're not sure it will generate enough money)? What would you like to be different in your next job than the past ones? The Authentic Vocation process described at *www.authenticvocation.com* can help you here, as can a career coach (directory available at *www.careercoachinstitute.com*).

- **Once your goal is clear, test it to be sure it is viable.** Are there enough jobs in that industry and position in the geographic area in which you want to work? If not, could you work remotely via computer, Internet, and phone and still achieve your goal?
- **Develop a job search plan.** One thing that has changed in job searching is that merely responding to help-wanted ads in the newspaper—or even surfing job boards on the Internet and responding to them—is not as likely to get you a job as other strategies. These two tactics are designed to access the "published" job market—but only 15 percent of all jobs are found that way. The rest are within the "unpublished" job market and are accessed through strategic networking, effective mailings to targeted employers, and the like. Your job search plan should include an appropriate mix of published and unpublished strategies, depending on whether you are pursuing a position in an industry you have already worked in or not.
- **Use results-oriented accomplishment statements, not just a list of responsibilities.** One of the most common mistakes people make on their résumés is listing a long list of position titles and responsibilities, but not details about what they have done. Remember WIIFM—the screener wants to know "What's In It for Me?" That is, what have you done that could be valuable to them? So first, go back only ten years in details on your work history, summarizing prior to that; second, describe what you've done in accomplishment statement format: situation, action taken, and results achieved (sales made, dollars saved, morale improved, etc.).

- **Make your credentials generic if switching fields.** Company names, industry-specific terms, and acronyms have no place in a résumé that you are using to attract work in a new industry. Instead of "Achieved ABC-Bank's sales quota of $50,000 in XYZ Loan sales and supervised five banking services representatives," say "Achieved Fortune 500 financial institution's sales quota of $50,000 in product-specific sales and supervised five professionals." This removes the barrier of "no experience in our industry" when the screener is reviewing your résumé.
- **Consider creative work structures for your new retirement career.** Finally, don't get caught in the nine-to-five in-the-office trap! In retirement, you might want to consider virtual work from home, entrepreneurship, part-time or contract work, or even volunteering your time. Surf the Web for sites on working at home and virtual work—you really *can* have it your way, especially in retirement!

There are also a number of Web sites that can assist you in making the transition from working full-time to a full or partly retired life.

http://www.retire2enjoy.com/
covers the psychology of retirement and includes a list of books.

http://www.kayehealey.com.au/
is an Australian site offering information on transitioning into retirement.

http://www.agewave.com/
includes articles on the aging of the labor force and its impact on your life.

http://www.aarp.org/
has a host of articles, information, references, and so on, of great value to retirees.

AARP's Best Employers for Workers over 50: 2004 Honorees

Appendix 2 presents a list of "Best Employers for People over 50" provided by AARP in 2004. These companies recruit seniors for full-time as well as part-time and temporary positions.

Health-care companies, financial service companies, and educational institutions dominated the list of best employers in the 2005 list of Best Employers for Older Workers. If this continues to hold true it may be best to focus your efforts with these types of employers, particularly if you are looking for a full-time position. Visit *http://www.aarp.org/money/careers/employerresourcecenter/bestemployers/2005.html* to see the entire list for 2005.

Where Do Retirees Live?

Chapter Overview

- Where Will You Live?
- Cities and States Where Seniors Live
- Fall in New England
- Compare Costs of Living

It is often said that it is not where you live but how you live that is important. While this is certainly true, where you live, at least for seniors, very much determines how you live. Your lifestyle as a senior or retiree will depend on whether you live at home by yourself or with your spouse or with family, in a retirement community, in an assisted-living community or a nursing home, and so forth. Your lifestyle will also depend on where you live geographically and how close you will be living to friends and family who can assist you in times of need.

Where Will You Live?

The following list gives some generalizations about the housing options for seniors and retirees:

At home, if they are healthy enough to care for themselves or if a member of the family or caregiver lives with them or can visit as often as is necessary to maintain their health and well-being.

With a family member or friend.

In an assisted-living or retirement community. Traditionally these facilities offer additional care for seniors who can function independently. They offer assistance with both personal care and medical care.

In a continuing-care facility. These facilities are actually retirement homes that allow seniors to move into a nursing home on site when/if necessary.

In a nursing home. These facilities provide skilled medical care for seniors who are dependent on others for daily functions. They have medical staff available 24/7.

At home with home health-care services. Seniors who generally need constant assistance due to their age or because of some disability live in this type of arrangement.

Hospice services are appropriate for the terminally ill and are available from weekly visits to around-the-clock attendance or in a hospice facility. Hospice services are connected to and work with physicians and hospitals to provide a maximum amount of emotional support to both patient and family. Hospice care typically refrains from using extraordinary measures to prolong life, but focuses instead on alleviating pain.

According to the U.S. Census Bureau, Nevada showed the greatest percentage increase among all states in residents 65 years of age and older; this state was up 72 percent between 1990 and 2000. Next was Alaska at 60 percent, Arizona at 39 percent, and New Mexico at 30 percent.

Cities and States Where Seniors Live

Cities with double-digit growth rates for the 65+ population include Denver, San Antonio, and Phoenix. The largest growth by far is the Las Vegas area, where the 65+ population grew 86 percent between 1990 and 2000 (99,000 to 184,000).

Read *Retire in Style: 50 Affordable Places across America* by Warren Bland for more information. This book offers valuable tips including which states have no personal income taxes (Alaska, Nevada, Texas, etc.) and which states, like Texas, freeze school-district property taxes for homeowners at age 65. William H. Frey analyzed census data to come up with cities with the greatest percentage growth in populations for people age 65 and over:

Major Metro Areas Rank (cities over 1 million)
- Las Vegas
- Phoenix
- Austin-San Marcos
- Houston-Galveston
- Atlanta
- Orlando
- Sacramento
- Raleigh-Durham
- Denver-Boulder
- Dallas–Fort Worth

Small Metro Areas Rank (cities under 1 million)
- Yuma, AZ
- Naples, FL
- Anchorage, AK
- Myrtle Beach, SC
- Las Cruces, NM
- Fort Walton Beach, FL
- Flagstaff, AZ
- Wilmington, NC
- McAllen-Edinburg, TX

More retirees are "living nowhere" as they are RV enthusiasts; many have seasonal residences, living south in the winter and north in the summer. Others just use their RVs to travel to various destinations around the United States. If you wish to find more information on RVs, the nation's largest RV dealer can be found online at *http://freedomroads.com/*.

A 2004 survey by Economy.com showed the following cities as being the most affordable: Elmira, Jamestown, Syracuse, Buffalo, Rochester, and Binghamton, New York; Springfield, Illinois; South Bend and Fort Wayne, Indiana; and Topeka, Kansas.

Many retirees choose to move north of the border as housing and the cost of living in most areas are less expensive, and there is a favorable exchange rate. However, Canada has stringent requirements for establishing residency. You must show good-sized net worth, pay a great deal of taxes, and, if you are intent on emigrating, a substantial amount of paperwork and up to three years waiting time.

Fall in New England
A friend of mine from college, Larry Morse, lives in New England and loves the northern climate all year round. For those of you thinking of moving south, there are also many good reasons to move north. I have included what Larry wrote about the coming of fall in New England. It reads like a poem. I loved what he said and have included it (see Appendix 1).

Compare Costs of Living
To compare the cost of living in your current location to the cost of living somewhere else, check out the Moving Calculator at *http://www.homestore.com* and the Salary Comparison Calculator at *http://www.monstermoving.com*. To find out how Americans by age group spend their money, see Figure 2.1.

Figure 2.1
Average Expenditures for Americans

Attributes	All households	< 50[1]	50+	55+	65+
Percent who are homeowners	67%	57%	80%	81%	83%
Percent of homeowners with a mortgage	61%	81%	43%	36%	21%
Average # of people in household	2.1	2.9	2	1.9	1.7
Annual spending per household					
Food	$5,340	$5,643	$4,940	$4,581	$3,896
Housing	$13,432	$14,403	$12,204	$11,402	$9,729
Furniture	$401	$460	$326	$294	$184
Major appliances	$196	$200	$190	$193	$165
Small appliances, dinnerware, cookware	$88	$81	$97	$90	$63
Sheet, towels, other household textiles	$113	$108	$121	$111	$90
Apparel	$1,640	$1,870	$1,342	$1,182	$908
Transportation	$7,781	$8,354	$7,055	$6,443	$4,824
New vehicles	$2,052	$2,055	$2,050	$2,025	$1,591
Old vehicles	$1,611	$1,904	$1,242	$1,060	$637
Health care	$2,416	$1,758	$3,250	$3,455	$3,741
Drugs	$467	$266	$722	$788	$905
Entertainment	$2,060	$2,142	$1,955	$1,865	$1,469
Insurance and pension expense[2]	$4,055	$4,505	$3,486	$2,749	$1,251
Other expenses	$4,093	$3,956	$4,267	$3,916	$3,558
Total	$40,817	$42,631	$38,499	$35,593	$29,376

Source: *Advertising Age's* American Demographics, based on Bureau of Labor Statistics' 2003 Consumer Expenditure survey. (1) Age reflects age of the homeowner or renter as identified by survey respondent. (2) Includes social security contribution (excludes health insurance, which is classified as health-care expense).

Start Your Home Office

Chapter Overview

- Setting Up
- Your Desk and Chair
- Telephone
- Computer Workstation
- Shredder
- File Cabinet
- Cards, Letterhead, Stationery
- Checklist of Miscellaneous Things to Have on Hand

You've probably had a desk/area at home where you have paid bills and handled personal business and will need to expand this area when you retire anyway. If you decide to have a home office, you will have to have a conversation with your spouse as you no doubt will be taking up additional space. I started with a home office myself, but as I expanded the space I quickly ran into difficulties with my wife and ended up renting a desk at the office of friends not far away.

If you have the space, it would be better if you could set up a separate room for your home office. This room should have a regular desk, a computer station, and all the things that are necessary for a home office. If you don't have enough space to devote a separate room, you could arrange a corner of the room where your business is conducted.

Setting Up
This will take a little time to make sure you have the appropriate working space in which to conduct your business. It could take weeks for you to do the entire setup with all the materials and equipment you will need. Places like Staples and Office Depot should have just about everything you will need. Local print shops like Insta-Print, Kinko's, and UPS Stores will also become important places to visit.

Your Desk and Chair
Perhaps the most important single item to find is a comfortable desk chair. You will be spending a fair amount of time in this chair, so don't skimp. Older backs and necks give all kinds of problems, and the "right" chair will minimize them. Whatever you do, don't use a handy chair that you have lying around your place. I know a number of people who have done this and regretted it later.

As far as the desk is concerned, you may be able to use the one that you already have. If not, you can either purchase a used one from the many used office furniture stores or a new one from an office supply store.

The lists that follow may seem obvious, but I've included them more or less as checklists.

Top of the desk
  Telephone
  Inbox/outbox
  Carrier for pens, pencils, hi-liters
  Post-it Note pads
  Scotch tape dispenser
  Blotter or desk pad
  Calculator
  Stapler
  Desk lamp (unless you use another source of light)
  Date book/calendar (some people use a calendar as a desk pad)
  Rolodex
  Alphabetized box for business cards you will collect/receive

Top middle drawer
  Current correspondence, checkbook, stamps, credit card receipts, things pending, bank statements

Top side drawer #1
  A tray to hold paper clips, rubber bands, staple remover, Wite-Out®, measuring tape, erasers, scissors

Top side drawer #2
  Extra batteries of all types you may need, extra printer ink cartridge, some small tools like a screwdriver (regular and Phillips head), box cutter, pliers, etc.

Drawer #3
  Letterhead, envelopes, extra paper for your printer, business cards, a few miscellaneous birthday cards, get-well cards, etc., for emergencies

Drawer #4
  Brochures, mail you have received of all kinds that you need not answer but wish to keep for reference

Telephone

It is important to get a second line. More problems develop working out of your home if you use your home phone for business. Arrange for a separate bill from your home phone, and make sure to include voice mail. Some phones also include fax capabilities if your copy machine does not. Incoming faxes can come via CallWave® 1-888-892-0021, which supplies you with a special fax number. All faxes come to your computer and can be printed on your printer. CallWave® can't be used for outgoing faxes.

Computer Workstation

You can, of course, use your PC or Mac, either a desktop or laptop model. If you find you need more than one computer, you can go online to research where you can get the best price for an additional unit or to the local computer or office supply store.

To go along with your computer you will need a copier/printer/scanner. New inkjet units are very inexpensive and can accomplish all of these tasks. The cost varies, but depending on what you want and where you make the purchase, it should run $68 to $250. I got mine at Costco for $68, and it works like a dream. Your computer station/area should have a place where you can store important books including telephone books, directories, an atlas, a dictionary, a thesaurus, and so on.

You should also have a box to keep discs (both blank and including information and back-up).

Shredder

Unfortunately with the large amount of identify theft you will need a shredder. They are inexpensive and can be purchased at almost any office supply store. Not only should you shred documents with personal information, but you should also shred all preapproved credit card solicitations.

File Cabinet

Whatever size file cabinet you purchase will probably fill up before you know it.

If the area in which you have your home office is small, you will probably have to make do with a small two-drawer. If you have the room, get a larger one as this will become the repository for all kinds of materials. Each year you will have to clean out the file cabinet, or you will be purchasing new ones regularly.

I would urge you to take the time to set up an organizing system for your files. You can purchase many different kinds of organizers at the local office supply store. Do so and it will save you a great deal of frustration later on.

Areas to organize:
- Revenue: gains and losses
- Expenses
- Other business deductions
- Insurance policies
- Insurance claims
- Medical/Medicare
- Purchases
- Contributions
- Tax forms and records
- Wills and legal documents

Cards, Letterhead, Stationery

The cost for these materials is surprisingly little at your local print shop.

One tip is to order a small number of all three. Of course, the more you order, the less expensive each item is; however, you may change your mind a month or two after starting your home office business and will want to make these changes on your cards and other marketing materials. I have changed my cards several times in the past few years and still have a quantity of the old ones that I just can't get myself to throw away.

Checklist of Miscellaneous Things to Have on Hand

Some of these you may already have around your place, but it is a good idea to pick up extras or you may find that your spouse has appropriated your supplies and has secreted them elsewhere where you can't find them when you need them.

> File folders
> Envelopes: 9×6, 8½×11, 9×12 and some standard #10s with no printing on them
> Paper clips (standard, large, and alligator)
> Rubber bands
> Ruler
> Scissors
> Letter opener
> Memo paper/note pads
> Extra staples
> Extra Scotch tape
> Briefcase

4

Volunteering

Chapter Overview

- Personal Advantages of Volunteering
- Find Places to Volunteer
- Clinical Trials: Why Volunteer for Clinical Trials of Medical Treatments?
- Contact Information for Charities and Nonprofits

Personal Advantages of Volunteering

Volunteering is fun and rewarding, and it makes you feel that you are accomplishing something, that you are giving back to the community in which you live, and that you are helping people. Volunteering also gives you the opportunity to meet people, make new friends, and get out of the house. You can volunteer a day or two a week, or in some cases even a few hours a day. Of course, some seniors volunteer every day.

But remember, when you volunteer you should be prepared to help in any way the organization needs you. You don't necessarily get to choose the areas in which you will work or the time you can spend. Most seniors who volunteer have found volunteering to be very gratifying.

According to N. Morrow-Howell, J. Hinterlong, P. A. Rozario, and F. Tang, "Older adults who volunteer and who engage in more hours of volunteering report higher levels of well-being."

Find Places to Volunteer

The Web site *http://www.volunteermatch.org/* helps seniors find places to volunteer. Just enter your ZIP code, and you will see all kinds of local volunteer opportunities posted by charities and nonprofits. VolunteerMatch has helped hundreds of thousands find rewarding volunteer positions, and their site lists the actual numbers for the major cities as well as some of the organizations that are what they call "nonprofit partners."

Clinical Trials: Why Volunteer for Clinical Trials of Medical Treatments?

The Food and Drug Administration, or FDA, is part of the U.S. government. It is the FDA's job to make sure medical treatments are safe and effective for people to use. By taking part in a clinical trial, you can try a new treatment that may or may not be better than those already available. You can also contribute to better understanding of how the treatment works in people of different ethnic backgrounds and genders. Information from the U.S. Food and Drug Administration is available at *http://www.fda.gov/opacom/lowlit/cltr.html.*

What Is a Clinical Trial?
"Clinical trial" is the scientific term for a test or study of a drug or medical device in people. These tests are done to see if the drug or device is safe and effective for people to use. Doctors and other health professionals run the tests according to strict rules set by the Food and Drug Administration (FDA). The FDA sets the rules to make sure that people who agree to be in the studies are treated as safely as possible.

How Can I Find Out about Clinical Trials?
One good way to find out if there are any treatments in clinical trials that might help you is to ask your doctor. Other sources of information include the following:

> For cancer, call 1-800-4-CANCER (1-800-422-6237), or visit *http://cancertrials.nci.nih.gov/.*

> For AIDS and HIV, call 1-800-TRIALS-A (1-800-874-2572), or visit *http://aidsinfo.nih.gov.*

> For general information about clinical trials, call the FDA's Office of Special Health Issues at 301-827-4460, or visit *http://www.fda.gov/oashi/home.html.*

> For other clinical trials, visit *http://www.nih.gov/health/trials/index.htm.*

Contact Information for Charities and Nonprofits
Perhaps you are interested in volunteering for a charity or nonprofit, but don't know where to start.

Alzheimer's Association
  http://www.alz.org/
  Click on Volunteer.

American Cancer Society
http://www.cancer.org/docroot/GI/GI_0.asp
Site shows you how to get involved.

American Diabetes Association
http://www.diabetes.org/home.jsp
Click on Volunteer, then click on Sign me up.

American Foundation for AIDS Research
http://www.thebody.com/amfar/amfar.html
Click on Volunteer opportunities.

American Heart Association
http://www.americanheart.org/presenter.jhtml?identifier=1200000
Click on Local information and choose a state.

American Red Cross
http://www.redcross.org/services/volunteer/0,1082,0_325_,00.html
Contact local chapter or call 800-435-7669.

American Society for Prevention of Cruelty to Animals
http://www.aspca.org/site/PageServer
Enter "volunteer" in the search box.

Animal Welfare Institute
http://www.awionline.org/
E-mail them for volunteer information.

Arthritis Foundation
http://www.arthritis.org/
Click on Become a volunteer.

Boy Scouts of America
http://www.scouting.org/
Click on Site map, screen down to Volunteer opportunities.

CARE
http://www.careusa.org/?source=www.care.org
Click on Get involved.

Volunteering

Catholic Charities
http://www.catholiccharitiesusa.org/
Click on How to join.

Child Welfare League of America
http://www.cwla.org/
Click on Membership.

Girl Scouts of the USA
http://www.girlscouts.org/
Go to Search and type in "volunteer"

Greenpeace USA
http://www.greenpeaceusa.org/
Click on Get active.

Guide Dog Foundation
http://www.guidedog.org/Voluntr/voluntr.htm
Click on Volunteer programs.

Helen Keller Services for the Blind
http://www.helenkeller.org/
Click on Site map and then click on How to become a volunteer.

Jewish National Fund
http://www.jnf.org/site/PageServer?pagename=Donation_Opportunities
Click on Volunteer.

Make-A-Wish Foundation
http://www.wish.org/
Click on Volunteer.

Muscular Dystrophy Association
http://www.mdausa.org/
Go to Ways to help and click on Volunteer.

National Park Service
http://www.nps.gov/volunteer/
Volunteer in our parks.

NAACP
http://www.naacp.org/work/membership/volunteer.shtml
Click on Volunteer opportunities.

Natural Resources Defense Council (NRDC)
http://www.nrdc.org/siteMap/
Protecting our natural resources.

The Salvation Army
http://www.salvationarmysouth.org/about.htm
Background and history.

Memorial Sloan-Kettering Cancer Center
http://www.mskcc.org/mskcc/html/44.cfm
Go to How to help and click on Volunteer.

St. Jude Children's Research Hospital
http://www.stjude.org/
To volunteer, open *http://www.stjude.org/volunteers*.

United Way
http://national.unitedway.org/
Click on Volunteer opportunity.

For phone contact information see the list of charities and nonprofits in Appendix 2 starting on page 203.

Continue Your Education

Chapter Overview

- Auditing Classes
- Online Schools
- Programs Offered

Many seniors look forward to retiring and going back to school. Some desire to earn a degree they never had the chance to pursue when they were younger, but most just want to stimulate their minds and learn about those areas that have always been interesting to them.

Auditing Classes

A number of colleges and universities allow seniors to audit classes at a nominal charge or at no cost at all. More and more retirees are taking advantage of these programs. Some universities have had to cap the number of auditing students to keep from flooding popular classes. A growing number of retirement communities have negotiated arrangements with nearby campuses as one of the benefits of living there.

Some of the larger programs include Boston University, where more than one thousand seniors a year audit classes through their Evergreen program. Seniors pay $50 a course. Colleges like Pomona and Penn State offer seniors the opportunity to audit classes free, while the University of Washington charges $5 per course. Some states like Minnesota and Virginia require in-state universities to allow seniors to audit classes.

Allowing seniors to audit classes is a win/win for both parties. Many seniors make financial gifts and some include the college in their wills. It is also excellent PR and helps to better integrate the college into the surrounding community in addition to providing an excellent marketing tool.

For a partial list of colleges and universities that allow auditing of classes go to *http://www.google.com* and enter "audit classes" in the advanced search box.

Online Schools

In addition to being able to audit classes where no college credit is given, many seniors are continuing their education at online schools. Below is a list of the top 10 by size:

University of Phoenix
AIU Online
Kaplan College Online
DeVry
Ellis MBA
Keiser College
Keller
Capella University
University of Cincinnati Online
Strayer University

You can reach these schools directly or go to *http://www.retiredbrains.com/Education/Index/* and search by industry, program, or state for the schools that best match your area of interest. This site also gives a brief description of the schools as well as a complete alphabetized listing of schools (copied below) and the degrees they offer (associates, bachelors, masters, diploma/certificate) with links to each.

Academy of Art College
http://www.retiredbrains.com/Education/Index/Form/SchoolForm.asp?GCD=&ICD=AAC&DOM

Advanced Technology Institute
http://www.retiredbrains.com/Education/Index/Form/SchoolForm.asp?GCD=&ICD=ADV&DOM=

AIU Online
http://www.retiredbrains.com/Education/Index/Form/SchoolForm.asp?GCD=&ICD=AIU&DOM=

Allied Medical & Technical Institute
http://www.retiredbrains.com/Education/Index/Form/SchoolForm.asp?GCD=&ICD=BTI&DOM=

Amarillo College of Beauty
http://www.retiredbrains.com/Education/Index/Form/SchoolForm.asp?GCD=&ICD=ACB&DOM=

American Graduate School of Management
http://www.retiredbrains.com/Education/Index/Form/ SchoolForm.asp?GCD=&ICD=AGS&DOM=

American Institute for Paralegal Studies, Inc.
http://www.retiredbrains.com/Education/Index/Form/ SchoolForm.asp?GCD=&ICD=APS&DOM=

Arizona Automotive Institute-Air Conditioning
http://www.retiredbrains.com/Education/Index/Form/ SchoolForm.asp?GCD=&ICD=AAI&DOM=

Ayers Institute
http://www.retiredbrains.com/Education/Index/Form/ SchoolForm.asp?GCD=&ICD=AYI&DOM=

Bauder College—Atlanta
http://www.retiredbrains.com/Education/Index/Form/ SchoolForm.asp?GCD=&ICD=BAU&DOM=

Berdan Institute
http://www.retiredbrains.com/Education/Index/Form/ SchoolForm.asp?GCD=&ICD=BRD&DOM=

Berks Technical Institute
http://www.retiredbrains.com/Education/Index/Form/ SchoolForm.asp?GCD=&ICD=BRK&DOM=

Boheckers Business College
http://www.retiredbrains.com/Education/Index/Form/ SchoolForm.asp?GCD=&ICD=BBC&DOM=

Bradley Academy of Arts—York
http://www.retiredbrains.com/Education/Index/Form/ SchoolForm.asp?GCD=&ICD=BAA&DOM=

Briarcliffe College—Patchogue
http://www.retiredbrains.com/Education/Index/Form/ SchoolForm.asp?GCD=&ICD=BRP&DOM=

California Design College
http://www.retiredbrains.com/Education/Index/Form/ SchoolForm.asp?GCD=&ICD=CDC&DOM=

Continue Your Education

Canadian Business College
http://www.retiredbrains.com/Education/Index/Form/SchoolForm.asp?GCD=&ICD=CAB&DOM=

Capella University
http://www.retiredbrains.com/Education/Index/Form/SchoolForm.asp?GCD=&ICD=CAP&DOM=

Career Networks Institute
http://www.retiredbrains.com/Education/Index/Form/SchoolForm.asp?GCD=&ICD=CNI&DOM=

Center for Certification and Adult Learning
http://www.retiredbrains.com/Education/Index/Form/SchoolForm.asp?GCD=&ICD=ADL&DOM=

Clarita Career College
http://www.retiredbrains.com/Education/Index/Form/SchoolForm.asp?GCD=&ICD=CLR&DOM=

Collins College
http://www.retiredbrains.com/Education/Index/Form/SchoolForm.asp?GCD=&ICD=COL&DOM=

Connecticut Center for Massage Therapy
http://www.retiredbrains.com/Education/Index/Form/SchoolForm.asp?GCD=&ICD=CMT&DOM=

Connecticut School of Electronics
http://www.retiredbrains.com/Education/Index/Form/SchoolForm.asp?GCD=&ICD=CSE&DOM=

Culinary Academy of Long Island
http://www.retiredbrains.com/Education/Index/Form/SchoolForm.asp?GCD=&ICD=CLI&DOM=

Daymar College—Owensboro
http://www.retiredbrains.com/Education/Index/Form/SchoolForm.asp?GCD=&ICD=DAY&DOM=

Denver Career College
http://www.retiredbrains.com/Education/Index/Form/SchoolForm.asp?GCD=&ICD=DCC&DOM=

Duffs Business Institute
http://www.retiredbrains.com/Education/Index/Form/SchoolForm.asp?GCD=&ICD=DUF&DOM=

Duluth Business University
http://www.retiredbrains.com/Education/Index/Form/SchoolForm.asp?GCD=&ICD=DBU&DOM=

Eagles Gate College
http://www.retiredbrains.com/Education/Index/Form/SchoolForm.asp?GCD=&ICD=EGC&DOM=

Edutech Centers—Clearwater
http://www.retiredbrains.com/Education/Index/Form/SchoolForm.asp?GCD=&ICD=ETC&DOM=

Electronic Institutes
http://www.retiredbrains.com/Education/Index/Form/SchoolForm.asp?GCD=&ICD=ELI&DOM=

Empire College
http://www.retiredbrains.com/Education/Index/Form/SchoolForm.asp?GCD=&ICD=EMP&DOM=

Everest College—Dallas
http://www.retiredbrains.com/Education/Index/Form/SchoolForm.asp?GCD=&ICD=EV1&DOM=

Everest College—Phoenix
http://www.retiredbrains.com/Education/Index/Form/SchoolForm.asp?GCD=&ICD=EV2&DOM=

Everest College—Rancho Cucamonga
http://www.retiredbrains.com/Education/Index/Form/SchoolForm.asp?GCD=&ICD=EV3&DOM=

Florida Career Institute
http://www.retiredbrains.com/Education/Index/Form/SchoolForm.asp?GCD=&ICD=FCI&DOM=

Florida Metropolitan University—Orange Park
http://www.retiredbrains.com/Education/Index/Form/SchoolForm.asp?GCD=&ICD=F01&DOM=

Fox College—Certificate Program
*http://www.retiredbrains.com/Education/Index/Form/
SchoolForm.asp?GCD=&ICD=FOX&DOM=*

Hagerstown College
*http://www.retiredbrains.com/Education/Index/Form/
SchoolForm.asp?GCD=&ICD=HAG&DOM=*

Hamrick Truck Driving School
*http://www.retiredbrains.com/Education/Index/Form/
SchoolForm.asp?GCD=&ICD=HMT&DOM=*

Hesser College—Manchester
*http://www.retiredbrains.com/Education/Index/Form/
SchoolForm.asp?GCD=&ICD=HSS&DOM=*

Hickey College—St. Louis
*http://www.retiredbrains.com/Education/Index/Form/
SchoolForm.asp?GCD=&ICD=HCK&DOM=*

Hunter Business School
*http://www.retiredbrains.com/Education/Index/Form/
SchoolForm.asp?GCD=&ICD=HTR&DOM=*

IBC—Fort Wayne
*http://www.retiredbrains.com/Education/Index/Form/
SchoolForm.asp?GCD=&ICD=IBC&DOM=*

ICT College—Los Angeles, CA Campus
*http://www.retiredbrains.com/Education/Index/Form/
SchoolForm.asp?GCD=&ICD=ICT&DOM=*

Institute for Business and Technology
*http://www.retiredbrains.com/Education/Index/Form/
SchoolForm.asp?GCD=&ICD=IBT&DOM=*

Institute of Business and Medical Careers
*http://www.retiredbrains.com/Education/Index/Form/
SchoolForm.asp?GCD=&ICD=IBM&DOM=*

IntelliTec College
*http://www.retiredbrains.com/Education/Index/Form/
SchoolForm.asp?GCD=&ICD=ITC&DOM=*

Interactive College of Technology
http://www.retiredbrains.com/Education/Index/Form/ SchoolForm.asp?GCD=&ICD=INT&DOM=

International Business College—Indianapolis
http://www.retiredbrains.com/Education/Index/Form/ SchoolForm.asp?GCD=&ICD=INB&DOM=

Internetwork Learning Institute
http://www.retiredbrains.com/Education/Index/Form/ SchoolForm.asp?GCD=&ICD=ILI&DOM=

Island Drafting and Technical Institute
http://www.retiredbrains.com/Education/Index/Form/ SchoolForm.asp?GCD=&ICD=ITD&DOM=

ITT Online & Campus
http://www.retiredbrains.com/Education/Index/Form/ SchoolForm.asp?GCD=&ICD=ITT&DOM=

Javelin Technical Training Center
http://www.retiredbrains.com/Education/Index/Form/ SchoolForm.asp?GCD=&ICD=JVT&DOM=

Keller Graduate School of Management
http://www.retiredbrains.com/Education/Index/Form/ SchoolForm.asp?GCD=&ICD=KEL&DOM=

Kings College—Charlotte
http://www.retiredbrains.com/Education/Index/Form/ SchoolForm.asp?GCD=&ICD=KNG&DOM=

Las Vegas College
http://www.retiredbrains.com/Education/Index/Form/ SchoolForm.asp?GCD=&ICD=LVC&DOM=

LaSalle Computer Learning Center
http://www.retiredbrains.com/Education/Index/Form/ SchoolForm.asp?GCD=&ICD=LAS&DOM=

Madison Media Institute
http://www.retiredbrains.com/Education/Index/Form/ SchoolForm.asp?GCD=&ICD=MAD&DOM=

Medix School
http://www.retiredbrains.com/Education/Index/Form/ SchoolForm.asp?GCD=&ICD=MDX&DOM=

Michigan Institute of Aeronautics
http://www.retiredbrains.com/Education/Index/Form/ SchoolForm.asp?GCD=&ICD=MIA&DOM=

Microskills
http://www.retiredbrains.com/Education/Index/Form/ SchoolForm.asp?GCD=&ICD=MSK&DOM=

Minneapolis Business College—Minneapolis
http://www.retiredbrains.com/Education/Index/Form/ SchoolForm.asp?GCD=&ICD=MBC&DOM=

Minnesota School of Business
http://www.retiredbrains.com/Education/Index/Form/ SchoolForm.asp?GCD=&ICD=MSB&DOM=

Missouri College
http://www.retiredbrains.com/Education/Index/Form/ SchoolForm.asp?GCD=&ICD=MSC&DOM=

Modern Technology College
http://www.retiredbrains.com/Education/Index/Form/ SchoolForm.asp?GCD=&ICD=MTC&DOM=

Mountain West College
http://www.retiredbrains.com/Education/Index/Form/ SchoolForm.asp?GCD=&ICD=MWC&DOM=

National Career Education
http://www.retiredbrains.com/Education/Index/Form/ SchoolForm.asp?GCD=&ICD=NCE&DOM=

National Heavy Equipment Operator School
http://www.retiredbrains.com/Education/Index/Form/ SchoolForm.asp?GCD=&ICD=NHE&DOM=

National Holistic Institute
http://www.retiredbrains.com/Education/Index/Form/ SchoolForm.asp?GCD=&ICD=NHI&DOM=

National Truck Drivers School
*http://www.retiredbrains.com/Education/Index/Form/
SchoolForm.asp?GCD=&ICD=NR3&DOM=*

Nevada Career Academy
*http://www.retiredbrains.com/Education/Index/Form/
SchoolForm.asp?GCD=&ICD=NCA&DOM=*

New Castle School of Trades
*http://www.retiredbrains.com/Education/Index/Form/
SchoolForm.asp?GCD=&ICD=NCS&DOM=*

NewSchool of Architecture and Design—San Diego
*http://www.retiredbrains.com/Education/Index/Form/
SchoolForm.asp?GCD=&ICD=NAD&DOM=*

Northern Westchester School of Hairdressing
*http://www.retiredbrains.com/Education/Index/Form/
SchoolForm.asp?GCD=&ICD=NWS&DOM=*

Northwest Technical College
*http://www.retiredbrains.com/Education/Index/Form/
SchoolForm.asp?GCD=&ICD=SEA&DOM=*

Ohio Institute of Photography & Technology
*http://www.retiredbrains.com/Education/Index/Form/
SchoolForm.asp?GCD=&ICD=OAK&DOM=*

PC Age
*http://www.retiredbrains.com/Education/Index/Form/
SchoolForm.asp?GCD=&ICD=PCA&DOM=*

Pima Community College/American Institute of Tech
*http://www.retiredbrains.com/Education/Index/Form/
SchoolForm.asp?GCD=&ICD=PIM&DOM=*

Pioneer Pacific College
*http://www.retiredbrains.com/Education/Index/Form/
SchoolForm.asp?GCD=&ICD=PPC&DOM=*

Professional Driver Institute
*http://www.retiredbrains.com/Education/Index/Form/
SchoolForm.asp?GCD=&ICD=PDI&DOM=*

Rochester Business Institute
*http://www.retiredbrains.com/Education/Index/Form/
SchoolForm.asp?GCD=&ICD=RBI&DOM=*

Samra University of Oriental Medicine
*http://www.retiredbrains.com/Education/Index/Form/
SchoolForm.asp?GCD=&ICD=SUO&DOM=*

Santa Barbara Business College
*http://www.retiredbrains.com/Education/Index/Form/
SchoolForm.asp?GCD=&ICD=SBB&DOM=*

Schuylkill Institute of Business & Technology
*http://www.retiredbrains.com/Education/Index/Form/
SchoolForm.asp?GCD=&ICD=SIB&DOM=*

Software Education of America-Lynnwood
*http://www.retiredbrains.com/Education/Index/Form/
SchoolForm.asp?GCD=&ICD=SFT&DOM=*

Southwest Florida College
*http://www.retiredbrains.com/Education/Index/Form/
SchoolForm.asp?GCD=&ICD=SFC&DOM=*

Springfield College
*http://www.retiredbrains.com/Education/Index/Form/
SchoolForm.asp?GCD=&ICD=SPC&DOM=*

Suburban Technical School
*http://www.retiredbrains.com/Education/Index/Form/
SchoolForm.asp?GCD=&ICD=STI&DOM=*

Technical Career Institute
*http://www.retiredbrains.com/Education/Index/Form/
SchoolForm.asp?GCD=&ICD=TCI&DOM=*

The Academy of South Florida
*http://www.retiredbrains.com/Education/Index/Form/
SchoolForm.asp?GCD=&ICD=ASF&DOM=*

The Chubb Institute—Cherry Hill, NJ Campus
*http://www.retiredbrains.com/Education/Index/Form/
SchoolForm.asp?GCD=&ICD=CH1&DOM=*

The Chubb Institute—North Brunswick, NJ Campus
*http://www.retiredbrains.com/Education/Index/Form/
SchoolForm.asp?GCD=&ICD=CH2&DOM=*

The Chubb Institute—Parsippany, NJ Campus
*http://www.retiredbrains.com/Education/Index/Form/
SchoolForm.asp?GCD=&ICD=CH3&DOM=*

The Chubb Institute—Springfield, PA Campus
*http://www.retiredbrains.com/Education/Index/Form/
SchoolForm.asp?GCD=&ICD=CH5&DOM=*

The Chubb Institute—Chicago Campus
*http://www.retiredbrains.com/Education/Index/Form/
SchoolForm.asp?GCD=&ICD=CH7&DOM=*

The Illinois Institute of Art—Schaumburg
*http://www.retiredbrains.com/Education/Index/Form/
SchoolForm.asp?GCD=&ICD=ISA&DOM=*

University of Baltimore Online (Bachelors)
*http://www.retiredbrains.com/Education/Index/Form/
SchoolForm.asp?GCD=&ICD=UBB&DOM=*

University of Baltimore Online (MBA)
*http://www.retiredbrains.com/Education/Index/Form/
SchoolForm.asp?GCD=&ICD=UBM&DOM=*

University of Baltimore Online (MPA)
*http://www.retiredbrains.com/Education/Index/Form/
SchoolForm.asp?GCD=&ICD=UBP&DOM=*

University of Phoenix Campus Programs
*http://www.retiredbrains.com/Education/Index/Form/
SchoolForm.asp?GCD=&ICD=UP4&DOM=*

University of Phoenix Online
*http://www.retiredbrains.com/Education/Index/Form/
SchoolForm.asp?GCD=&ICD=UP8&DOM=*

Valencia Institute
*http://www.retiredbrains.com/Education/Index/Form/
SchoolForm.asp?GCD=&ICD=VAL&DOM=*

Continue Your Education

Wood Tobe Coburn—New York
http://www.retiredbrains.com/Education/Index/Form/
SchoolForm.asp?GCD=&ICD=WTC&DOM=

WyoTech—Boston
http://www.retiredbrains.com/Education/Index/Form/
SchoolForm.asp?GCD=&ICD=EAT&DOM=

York Technical Institute
http://www.retiredbrains.com/Education/Index/Form/
SchoolForm.asp?GCD=&ICD=YTI&DOM=

Below is a list of some of the programs offered:

Accounting
http://www.retiredbrains.com/Education/Index/Results
.asp?PID=2143&PNM=Accounting&DOM=

Administrative assistant
http://www.retiredbrains.com/Education/Index/Results
.asp?PID=2144&PNM=Administrative%20Assistant&
DOM=

Air conditioning, refrigeration and heating
http://www.retiredbrains.com/Education/Index/Results
.asp?PID=2145&PNM=Air%20Conditioning,%20Refrig
eration%20and%20Heating&DOM=

Architecture and drafting
http://www.retiredbrains.com/Education/Index/Results
.asp?PID=2146&PNM=Architecture%20and%20Draft
ing&DOM=

Business administration
http://www.retiredbrains.com/Education/Index/Results
.asp?PID=2147&PNM=Business%20Administration&
DOM=

Business applications
http://www.retiredbrains.com/Education/Index/Results
.asp?PID=2148&PNM=Business%20Applications&
DOM=

Cisco certification
*http://www.retiredbrains.com/Education/Index/Results
.asp?PID=2149&PNM=Cisco%20Certification&DOM=*

Information technology certification
*http://www.retiredbrains.com/Education/Index/Results
.asp?PID=2165&PNM=Information%20Technology%20
Certification&DOM=*

Information technology management
*http://www.retiredbrains.com/Education/Index/Results
.asp?PID=2166&PNM=Information%20Technology%20
Management&DOM=*

Law enforcement, security, and criminal justice
*http://www.retiredbrains.com/Education/Index/Results
.asp?PID=2167&PNM=Law%20Enforcement,%20Secur
ity%20and%20Criminal%20Justice&DOM=*

Legal services
*http://www.retiredbrains.com/Education/Index/Results
.asp?PID=2179&PNM=Legal%20Services&DOM=*

Maintenance and repair
*http://www.retiredbrains.com/Education/Index/Results
.asp?PID=2168&PNM=Maintenance%20and%20Repair
&DOM=*

Management
*http://www.retiredbrains.com/Education/Index/Results
.asp?PID=2169&PNM=Management&DOM=*

Marketing and advertising
*http://www.retiredbrains.com/Education/Index/Results
.asp?PID=2170&PNM=Marketing%20and%20Advertisi
ng&DOM=*

Medical billing and coding
*http://www.retiredbrains.com/Education/Index/Results
.asp?PID=2171&PNM=Medical%20Billing%20and%20
Coding&DOM=*

Medical technologist
http://www.retiredbrains.com/Education/Index/Results.asp?PID=2172&PNM=Medical%20Technologist&DOM=

Microsoft certification
http://www.retiredbrains.com/Education/Index/Results.asp?PID=2173&PNM=Microsoft%20Certification&DOM=

Network administration
http://www.retiredbrains.com/Education/Index/Results.asp?PID=2174&PNM=Network%20Administration&DOM=

Network security
http://www.retiredbrains.com/Education/Index/Results.asp?PID=2175&PNM=Network%20Security&DOM=

Network technology
http://www.retiredbrains.com/Education/Index/Results.asp?PID=2176&PNM=Network%20Technology&DOM=

Nursing
http://www.retiredbrains.com/Education/Index/Results.asp?PID=2177&PNM=Nursing&DOM=

Oracle
http://www.retiredbrains.com/Education/Index/Results.asp?PID=2178&PNM=Oracle&DOM=

Personal care services
http://www.retiredbrains.com/Education/Index/Results.asp?PID=2180&PNM=Personal%20Care%20Services&DOM=

Trades
http://www.retiredbrains.com/Education/Index/Results.asp?PID=2181&PNM=Trades&DOM=

Transportation and heavy equipment training
*http://www.retiredbrains.com/Education/Index/Results
.asp?PID=2182&PNM=Transportation%20and%20
Heavy%20Equipment%20Training&DOM=*

Travel and tourism
*http://www.retiredbrains.com/Education/Index/Results
.asp?PID=2183&PNM=Travel%20and%20Tourism&
DOM=*

Web design
*http://www.retiredbrains.com/Education/Index/Results
.asp?PID=2184&PNM=Web%20Design&DOM=*

6

Become Computer Literate

Chapter Overview

- What Can You Use the Internet to Do?
- Using a Computer Is Easy
- E-mail for Beginners—Everything You Need to Get Started
- How To: A Computer Primer
- Where You Can Go to Get Instruction
- Books You Can Purchase

Seniors are the fastest-growing age group becoming Internet literate, according to Nielsen/NetRatings. The number of seniors using Internet sites like eBay to buy and sell merchandise has grown substantially in just the past year. Seniors are also using search engines like Google and Yahoo to gather information, but the largest increase in Internet use by seniors is the use of e-mail. Many grandparents use e-mail because they want to better communicate with their grandchildren. When you call Billy or Nancy on the phone, what you usually hear after less than a minute is "Gotta go, now, Grandpa. Here's Mom." With e-mail or even instant messaging, you have a great way to interact more with your grandchildren... on their terms.

So if you have not started learning how to use a computer, you need to *start learning now*. If you are able to e-mail, but can't do much more than send and receive, you should *start learning more now*.

Don't let computers threaten you. They are really quite nice and easy to use, even if you have absolutely no technical knowledge at all. Hopefully what you read in this chapter can get you started.

What Can You Use the Internet to Do?

I have listed only a few of the many areas.

- Communicate by e-mail (see "E-mail for Beginners" below)
- Study and research
- Read online newspapers, magazines, and publications
- Play games and "stuff"
- Access course material on almost every subject
- Receive newsletters in areas of interest
- Purchase products and services
- Compare prices of products and services
- Sell products and services
- View entertainment features

Using a Computer Is Easy

A 2004 survey from the Pew Internet and American Life Project shows that 22 percent of Americans 65 and older, or roughly 8 million seniors, are already online. That number is expected to rise, as 58 percent of the age group 50–64 are already computer literate. Joining this group could be one of the most important decisions you make as a senior, and if so many other seniors have been able to do so, why are you so worried?

More than 250 sites cater specifically to seniors, and more on going online every day. Computer knowledge is key, as is evidenced by a study by the National Bureau of Economic Research, which showed that employees who maintain their computer technology skills retire later than those who don't embrace computing.

Most of the seniors I know are primarily interested in understanding how to use e-mail. Here are easy, step-by-step instructions you can easily follow once you have purchased a computer and have arranged for an Internet connection. Of course you could also start the learning process using a computer belonging to a friend or family member, and they might even help you with the basics.

E-mail for Beginners—
Everything You Need to Get Started

Diana Rasbid is the author of the best article I have found that helps seniors become computer literate and learn how to use the Internet. I have included her helpful instructions below:

> This information is not intended to be the sole and exclusive definition of the contents covered but rather a helpful series of signposts and maps to guide your way. With the exponential number of versions of Microsoft Windows, Microsoft Word, other operating systems and word processing programs it is impossible to cover every single variation and combination

of instructions. These instructions were written using Microsoft Windows XP Home Edition and Microsoft Word 2000. Macintosh is not covered at all in this chapter. Folder and file pathways may be different, as may pop-up instruction windows, etc.

So you have the computer, you've got access to the Internet, there are lots of buttons and icons on the screen, and it's just all too much. The following instructions are written with these assumptions:

You know how to open your e-mail program on the computer and that it is configured to send and receive.

You know what a mouse is and how to point, click, and double-click on the screen with some degree of dexterity.

If you are at that point, read on.

Many different e-mail programs allow you to communicate around the globe or down the street. They include PC-based programs such as Microsoft Outlook, and Web-based ones such as Hotmail, Yahoo, AIM, and G-mail. The layout is different on all of them, but the basic functions remain the same. I am going to use Outlook as my model as it is a very commonly installed mail program. Take a deep breath, and here we go.

I am only going to deal with sending and receiving mail and adding and receiving attachments, as these are the four functions most seniors want to use. You want to be able to keep in touch with your grandkids and adult children, and there are all those photos to look at that they keep sending you and you just can't seem to open. When you tell your 10-year-old grandkid that you couldn't view the picture of them hitting the home run, they just take the mouse from you and clickety-click a few times and, *Voila*, the picture is on your screen. Frustrating? You bet! So make yourself a hot or cold drink, get comfortable in front of that abominable piece of technology taking up your desk space, and open up your e-mail program.

Become Computer Literate 57

The square box that has opened on your screen is called a window. It should cover the whole screen area. If it doesn't, then you need to maximize the window. Look in the very top right of the window, and there are three small boxes. If you hover your mouse pointer over each one a little yellow box will pop up with a word in it. The underline in the box says Minimize, the square in the box says Maximize, and the red cross in the box says Close. Click your mouse pointer on the middle one a few times. It makes the window bigger and smaller. Clicking on the Minimize makes the window "slide" into the taskbar at the bottom. To get it back, click the Outlook bar at the bottom of the screen. It slides back up again. Now, maximize the window. When the window is maximized the middle button changes to a different one—two small squares, one in front of the other—and it says Restore Down.

The main Outlook window should automatically go to the Inbox view. There should be a row of words and a couple of rows of icons or buttons across the top of the window. Down the left-hand side there should be a folder list, and the main section of the page should be the list of e-mails you have in your inbox. If it is not exactly like that, don't panic.

The row of words at the top is called the menu bar and should read similar to: File, Edit, View, Favorites, Tools, Actions, Help. The word Help is your new best friend. *Use it.* I have been using computers for over twenty years and consider myself pretty adept, but I use the help menu with various programs every single day. That's what it is there for—to *help* you. There is a help menu for every decent piece of software on the market. Don't be afraid to ask questions there. At least the computer won't roll its eyes and look at you as if you are totally idiotic!

If you single-click your mouse pointer on the word File, it opens a drop-down menu. The first three words are New, Open, and Close. If you look to the left of the words, New and Open, both have an icon next to them. "New" is a blank sheet of paper, and "Open" is a yellow open folder. Let the file menu pop back up and look at the first row of buttons under the word File. You should see the New and Open buttons repeated there also. Many of the commands in the popups under the menu bar words are repeated as buttons on the toolbars. With time and familiarity you will be able to start using those buttons. If you are already doing so, that is fantastic. Don't have those little picture buttons on your screen? Single-click on the word View on the menu bar, go down to Toolbars, wait for a second for another menu to open to the side, slide across and then down to the word Formatting, and click. Now you should have buttons.

Look down to the left of your Outlook window. Is there a folder list showing a "tree" of the folders and subfolders in your e-mail? Not everyone likes to see the folder list, but for those new to the game it is handy to start with. If it is not there, single-click on the View menu at the top and go down to Folder List and click. It should be there now. There are various words there such as Calendar, Contacts, Deleted Items, Inbox, Outbox, Sent Items, and Tasks. Single-clicking on each one will show you the contents of each folder.

Let's send an e-mail to someone. Click again on Inbox. Now you either go to the File menu, down to New and across to Mail Message, and click. Or you might see the button New under the word File, which you can click. Both of these actions will open a new window titled Untitled Message. Again, this window may open up as a full screen window or as a small window where you can still see parts of the Inbox window behind it. Maximize the Untitled Message window so that it fills the screen. Use the little box at top right with the square in it. Having the message window fill the entire screen will help you not get confused by looking at buttons on the window behind.

The top of the message window is similar to the main Outlook window. The menu bar at the top with the word menus, the toolbar underneath with the buttons. Under that is the word Send with other buttons to the right, the word To, the letters Cc, and the word Subject. There may also be the let-

Become Computer Literate 59

ters Bcc if that is turned on. We will come back to that. So what does it all mean?

Send is pretty obvious—that is the button you are going to press to send the e-mail after you have written your letter and addressed it. To is who you are sending the mail to—their e-mail address. Cc means carbon copy, and you can send the same e-mail at the same time to many other people. All those people will be able to see all the other e-mail addresses so they should already know each other. It is very bad netiquette to Cc mail to people who don't know each other. Family should be fine!! Subject is the intro line—short and sweet, such as "Baseball pic of Little Jimmy." Don't make it too cryptic, and don't make it too long. Both are the mark of spammers. Bcc means Blind Carbon Copy and is similar to Cc except no one else can see anyone else's e-mail addresses.

The first thing you need to do is address the letter. Instead of an envelope and stamp, all you need is the e-mail address. All e-mail addresses follow the same pattern. There is a beginning, middle, and end. The beginning is the person's name or nickname or "handle," which can vary from as staid as johnsmith25 to purplemonkeybanana. The middle is the @ sign. You cannot put "at," even though that is what people say when they tell you their e-mail address; it must be the @ sign found above the number 2 on all keyboards. The end is the person's e-mail server name. It could be yahoo.com or dea.gov or sbcglobal.net or gdfb.org or any of myriad possibilities. The complete e-mail address should look something like this: dianabolton66@bigpond.com = username + @ + server. So now, type the address of the person you are going to send this e-mail to. You can address it to yourself if you like, as a test run to see just how clever you are.

We don't want to Cc anyone in this mail so leave the Cc line blank. The subject line should only be a few words. Not too cryptic—I got one titled "t a t" from my senior citizen father one day. Took me ages to work out he meant "this and that." Not too long-winded: "Here is the great pic of Little Jimmy hitting the home run to win the ninth. Look at the expression on his face!!!" Short and sweet—"Baseball pic of Little Jimmy" will do fine. So title your e-mail. If you are sending it to yourself, just "testing" will do.

Now the e-mail is addressed. Click in the body, the writing part, of the e-mail and write what you want to write. Use the standard salutations you would in any letter. If you always start with "My dearest Madeleine," then continue to do so. If you are more of a "hey folks" type of person, use that. Just be natural.

Now we are going to add an attachment. Hopefully you know how to "browse" your computer to find where you have stored all the photos of your grandkids. If you don't, "Houston, we have a problem!" First of all, make sure your cursor is in the body part of the e-mail, or this next bit won't work. Click anywhere in the text part of the e-mail. Then click on the Insert menu at the top on the menu bar, slide down to File, which is near the bottom, and click. You could also have done that by clicking the little paperclip near the word Send. This brings up a small window called Insert file. You need to browse the directory of your computer to where you have the pictures stored, then click the one you want to attach, and then click Insert at the bottom right of the Insert File window. If you don't have any pictures to send and are just doing a test, attach a Word document, maybe a poem you have written or a letter to the bank. It works just the same.

If you managed this step, you will now have another line below the Subject line, which says Attach, and next to it is the name of the file you just attached. You are now ready to send. This really is as simple as clicking the Send button on the e-mail. For those of you who have their computer set up to send and receive every five or ten minutes, you need to do nothing further. Outlook will store your e-mail in the Outbox until it next connects. But we are impatient creatures, so go ahead; let's make it go right now. Click the Send button. Oh, no! The e-mail has vanished. Don't panic, folks.

If you look over to the left at your folder list, you will see your e-mail sitting in the Outbox. If it is the only e-mail waiting to go, then the word Outbox will be highlighted in dark black and there will be (1) in blue next to it. Now, let's make it leave that Inbox and head off to cyberspace. Once again there are two ways to do this. You can either click the Send/Receive button on the toolbar or you can go to the Menu bar and click Tools, Send, and Receive. The button is always easier! Depending how your e-mail is configured you may be prompted for a password each time you send and receive. Or it may just happen automatically. Let's check if the e-mail went.

Look again at your folder list and find the Sent Items folder. Single-click Sent Items, and you can see the mail that has been sent from your computer. The one you just sent should be at the top of the list. If it isn't, you can sort your e-mails quickly by clicking on the words at the top of the list such as To, Subject, Sent. Just click To and see what happens. When you click next to the word, a little triangle appears. The list is sorted alphabetically A–Z. If you click the triangle again, it sorts Z–A. Click next to Subject, again alphabetically. I find it easiest to have them sorted by date as the default. Click next to Sent, and it sorts newest to oldest. Click again, and it reverses the sort.

So now you have sent e-mail and an attachment. Let's have a look at some e-mail you may have received, with attachments that you have been unable to open. If the one you just sent is the very first e-mail to have ever been sent or received that's fine—just stay in the Sent Items folder, and we will use that e-mail as an example. If you sent a test to yourself, it may not have come straight back to you when you Sent and Received. Sometimes there is a delay. So hit that Send/Receive button again and see if you have mail!

Receiving mail happens automatically when you press Send/Receive. Someone may have sent the mail last week, but it is stored on your mail server until you download it. (Often there is a time limit on that.) You know you have new mail when you can see e-mails in dark bold text in your inbox. On the far left of the line with the e-mail sender and subject and date there is a little icon. A yellow closed envelope means you haven't opened it. A white open envelope means you have. A maroon arrow on the opened envelope means you have replied to it, and a blue arrow means you forwarded the e-mail onto someone else.

Once you have mail in your inbox, how do you read it? Two ways. If you single-click the first e-mail, the whole line goes blue. Double-click that blue line, and the e-mail will open in a new window. Again, if it is a small window maximize the window at top right. Now you can read the text. The second way is through the preview pane. This allows you to read the e-mail in the main Outlook window without opening a new window for each e-mail. Some people like it, and some people don't. To turn it on, go to the Menu bar to View, slide down to Preview Pane, and click. Now the main body of the Inbox window has been split in half. If you single-click an e-mail in the top section you can then read it in the bottom section. If it is a long e-mail, you will have to scroll down to read it all—use the scroll bars at the right-hand side. If you just loathe this way of looking at your e-mail, turn it off the same way you turned it on: menu bar, View, Preview Pane, click.

How do you know if there is an attachment? Go to the sent items folder where you can see the e-mail you just sent. There are two little icons next to the e-mail. One is the open white envelope, and the other is a paperclip. Whenever you see a paperclip next to an e-mail, you know there is an attachment. Open that e-mail again by double-clicking the e-mail. You should now be able to see an icon at the bottom of the e-mail with the name of the attachment you sent. Different types of documents have different pictures in them. A Word document might have a W in the middle, for example. To look at the attachment, you double-click that icon. You may get a warning box telling you that opening files may give you a virus. If you are sure the file is from a trusted source (and you should have antivirus software anyway!) then click the dot next to Open it, not next to Save to disk, and then OK. The attachment will open in a new window.

Now if it is a picture, often the picture is in a format called a bitmap. Many people are not aware that they should resize their pictures down to something smaller and that they should always save them as a .jpg not a .bmp. So when you open these pictures, you may only be seeing the top left of the picture. Use the scrolling bars at right and bottom to see the rest of the picture.

If it is a text document it is most likely going to be a Microsoft Word document. Mostly these documents will open without any trouble, but every now and then someone will send you something that won't open, or if it does it is just hieroglyphic gibberish. This is not your fault.

Now it is practice time. You will make mistakes for certain. You will become frustrated and want to throw the machine out the window. Please persevere. Use the Help menu. Want to know what the Organize button means? Open up Help, type in the word you want defined, and hit Search. Have a go. Try new stuff. Once you have mastered e-mail the Internet is waiting. What a wealth of misinformation and garbage is out there! There is also an incredible plethora of "stuff" that you had no idea you needed to know. Above all, have fun.

How To: A Computer Primer

Here is a very simple alphabetical list of "How To" bits and pieces for use with e-mail, the Internet, and Word. It is by no means comprehensive or all-encompassing, but it might get you started with some new tricks.

ADDRESS BOOK—ENTERING NEW NAMES
  Open up Outlook Express by clicking the icon at the bottom of the screen.
  Either click Address Book button on toolbar **or** click Tools, scroll down to Address Book, and click.
  In Address Book window, Click File—New Contact **or** click New button and slide down to New Contact and click.

Type in Details in next window. Click Add when you have put in e-mail address. Click OK on same box.

NOTE: You can change alphabetical order from A to Z or Z to A in the address book list by clicking on the little arrow above the names.

ADDRESSES—on the WWW

Open up Internet Explorer, the "e" icon at bottom of screen.

When page is open click www. It goes blue.

Type the new www address. Press Enter on keyboard.

When it is at the correct site click Favorites *if* you want to add it to your favorites.

On the Favorites menu click Add to favorites.

Select folder where you want it to go by left-clicking once.

Click OK.

ADDRESSOR'S E-MAIL, HOW TO FILE

Get the required e-mail up on screen by double-clicking.

Single-right-click the person's name up, the top in the from line.

Click Add to Address Book from pop-up menu.

You can also Block Sender the same way by clicking Block Sender.

To change any details for the person, e.g. capitals or not, click on Address book in the main Outlook Window, double-click the person's name in the list, and edit in the new window. Click OK when finished.

ARROW, BLUE/GREEN, E-MAIL

Tells you that you have forwarded the sender's message to someone else.

ARROW, RED/PURPLE, E-MAIL

Tells you that you have replied to the sender's message.

BARS—BOTTOM

If bar at the *bottom* of the computer screen moves to the side or the top:

Left click in blank space on the bar, hold and drag back to the bottom.

BLANK SCREEN—see SCREEN GOES BLANK

BOXES/CROSSES—TOP RIGHT OF SCREEN—*with 'x' in middle*

If there are two boxes, one under the other, at the top right of the screen, then the top cross (red) is to close the program; the bottom cross is to close the file or document.

BULLETS

Same as under PARAGRAPHS—NUMBERING.

CHAPTER, NEW

Open WORD document.
Go to File, Save As.
Browse folder to where you want the document to go.
Name the document with new chapter name *exactly* as you have named the other.
Click Save.

CHARACTERS NOT ON KEYBOARD

Suppose you want to type "two and a half" numerically:
Type '2'.
Click Insert, scroll down to Symbol and left-click.
SYMBOL box appears.
Select font required. Use any font for normal symbols, letters and numbers; use Wingdings or Webdings for pictures.
Box full of symbols appears.
Browse for and click on the $1/2$.
Click on Insert. Click on Close.

CLICKING—'RIGHT'
Always get a pop-up menu from which you can select further options.
(Clicking left opens—or closes—something.)

CLICKS
One click moves the cursor to desired position.
Two clicks in middle of word selects that word.
Three clicks in middle of paragraph selects the line or whole paragraph.
When you hover in margin at start of line, an arrow will appear.
Then one click selects line; two clicks selects the paragraph.
Clicking and dragging selects more than one word or line or paragraph;
CTRL + A selects whole document—for "bold," for example.

COMPUTER ERROR—GROSS
If the computer goes seriously off-track you can reset it to how it was the week before. Go Start, and click Systems Restore on left column if this feature is turned on. This does not always achieve your aim anyway, and the feature is probably better left Off. System Restore uses a lot of your system memory.

COMPUTER FREEZES
Hold down Ctrl + Alt and then press Delete. Task Manager opens. Make sure Applications Tab is selected. If the program that has "hung" says "NOT RESPONDING" then click on End Task at bottom of box.
or Hold down Ctrl + Alt + Escape. This does the same thing.
or Hold down power button until it switches off. Wait thirty seconds and switch on again.

CTRL (CONTROL) ON KEYBOARD IN A WORD DOCUMENT

CTRL + A Enables whole document to be changed. Font, bold, underline, etc.

CTRL + B Make selected letters or words bold.

CTRL + D Gives Font box for changing all fonts formatting.

CTRL + C Copy selected text or object.

CTRL + I Makes letters *Italics*.

CTRL + O When writing, use to open up a new blank document.

CTRL + P Print document.

CTRL + S Save document. Only use when you have Saved As already.

CTRL + X Cut selected text or object.

CTRL + V Paste selected text or object.

CTRL + Z Undo the last action.

CUT, COPY, AND PASTE

Place cursor at start of writing (paragraph, line, whatever) to be shifted and select all you want shifted. When it is highlighted you can then use Cut or Copy, then move cursor to new position where text is to be inserted and Paste. Alternatively you can drag the text to the new position. Highlight text, left-click, and hold mouse click down. Drag. Move slowly and carefully.

To cut: Highlight text to be cut. Click on cut icon (scissors) on bar *or* CTRL + X.

To copy: Highlight text to be copied. Click on copy icon (two sheets of paper) on bar *or* CTRL + C.

To paste: Scroll to where you want writings to go and insert cursor at correct insertion point. Click on paste icon (clipboard) on bar *or* CTRL + V.

DESKTOP, ALTERING
   Right click in middle of desktop. Left click on Properties. Click Desktop tab. Choose picture from the list of browse directory to choose a picture you like and double-click it. Point onto Center and choose Stretch. Click Apply and OK.

DOCUMENTS, DELETING
   See: Writings, stored—deleting

DOCUMENTS, FINDING
   See: Writings, stored—finding

DOCUMENTS, FINDING, WHEN USING ONE ALREADY
   If already working on one document and wanting to get to another, click the yellow Folder button or File, Open. This enables you to select another document.

EDITING—'FIND,' 'REPLACE,' AND 'GO TO' (IN WORD)
   On the keyboard, use F5 *or* CTRL + F, *or* Edit, Find *or* Binocular Button.
   Each of these gets you to the Find and Replace window.
   You can find a word in a document—e.g., "Bossy Lady".
   You can replace that word or all instances of word with another—e.g., "Fierce Lady".
   You can go to a page within the document without scrolling.

E-MAIL—ATTACHMENT—INSERTING
   Open Outlook Express and click on Create New Mail button, or File, New Mail.
   Click Insert, File Attachment (on menu) or the attachment button (paperclip).
   Select files from directory and double-click to select just one of them.
   Or hold down CTRL and click on more than one if needed. Click Insert.

These files (one or more) appear on message.
Click Send.

E-MAIL—ATTACHMENTS—SAVING OR VIEWING
To read e-mail attachments and then file if desired:
Click paper clip on the right in e-mail preview page.
Click Save attachments only if you want to. Otherwise single-left-click on document name in order to open or read.

E-MAIL—BACKGROUNDS—TO MAKE STATIONERY LOOK PRETTY
Open Create Mail. Get New Message.
Go Format.
Go Apply Stationery—select one.
Click OK. Colors appear in message body.

E-MAIL—BLOCKING SENDER
Open up message you wish to block. Go to Message on top bar. Go Block Sender. Click Yes.

E-MAIL—CHECKING whether you have replied to or forwarded the e-mail:
Open Outlook Express—shortcut button down at bottom on taskbar.
In the Inbox or other Folder, the envelope:
Has a red arrow to show the message is replied to.
Has a blue arrow to show the message has been forwarded on to someone else.

E-MAIL—DELETING
Open Outlook Express and locate the list of folders down the left-hand side.
(If you are sure that you know what is in the Deleted Folder, then you can do the next step. If you are not sure, then click on Deleted Items and check that there are no e-mails in the folder that should not be deleted.)
If you are sure, Right click on Deleted Items.
Click on Empty Deleted Items folder. It prompts to make sure, click OK.

E-MAIL—DRAFTS—TO BE SENT LATER

When you have an e-mail on screen which you want to go into draft box to finish or send later, you must click File, Save. Then Click OK, *or* click cross at top right of e-mail and then OK.

When you wish to return to Draft to continue typing e-mail:

Click Draft folder at left. One or more messages will appear.

Double left-click message in window; it will open.

Make any alterations to e-mail. When you are satisfied it is ready to send, Click Send button.

(Note: you must have an address and a subject.)

E-MAIL—FORWARDING

If you have an e-mail you wish to send on to someone else:

Open e-mail. Click Forward button on top of e-mail.

Type in address of person to send it to or use Address Book.

Click Send.

E-MAIL—LETTERS—TO SEND AN ACTUAL WORD DOCUMENT

Create letter in Word—could use letterhead Ash Farm stationery—and save in a Folder, such as "Letters."

Open Outlook Express and Create a new e-mail. Address e-mail and put something in Subject line.

Click the attach icon (paperclip—you will have to maximize the e-mail to see the paperclip), or Insert, File Attachment from menu.

Browse for the letter document in the folder and double left-click to attach. Write anything in body of e-mail if you desire. Click Send.

E-MAIL—SENDING
Click Send, top left-hand corner of Message box.
On e-mail box, click Send/Receive.

ENVELOPE—WORD
Have letter/document open.
Highlight Address in document.
Go to Tools, then Envelopes and Labels, then Envelopes.
Or Click button on tool bar (small rectangle with address in it).
Put envelope sticky side down, and the stamp area away from you. Click Print.

FAVORITES—TO ENTER—only when at the www site chosen
On very top bar click on Favorites.
Click on Add on favorites.
Box appears. Write in name of favorite.
Next put it into Finance, Prose, or whatever and click OK.

FILE—DELETING
Select file. Click on delete icon on toolbar, or press Delete on keyboard.

FILE—FINDING
Hold down Start, Search or Windows key on keyboard and click F.
Click All Files and Folders.
Note: Windows + E gets you Explorer.
Make sure you are looking in the C drive.
Then type in file name.
Click Search.

FILE—OPENING
Click My Computer and browse directory to find file you need.
Double left-click—it opens.

FILE ON MENU BAR in WORD
Useful items: New, Open, Close, Save, Save as, Page setup, Print.

Note: Select All on Edit menu allows you to change Justification, Font, or whole article.

FILE OR FOLDER—RE-NAMING
Open My Computer.

From selected file, find item to be renamed and click on it.

Wait two seconds, and left-click again on name to renamed.

Name of file turns blue, and flashes.

Type new name on keyboard.

Click just outside icon/box—name changes, *or* hit Enter.

FILES—RE-ARRANGING
Open folder where file is.

Open folder to where file is going.

Left-click on file to be moved, hold and drag onto file into which you wish to move it.

Click F5 to refresh.

To Select More Than One File:
Left-click first file, and let go.

Hold Ctrl down.

Select all other files to shift, one at one time.

Let go Ctrl.

Click on one highlighted file or group of files and drag to Prose.

Let go.

FLOPPY DISKS, TO SAVE ONTO
Have the document open that you want to save onto floppy. Insert floppy disk into drive.

Click File, Save as.

Browse to floppy drive—click arrow next to Save in, and click 3^1/2 Floppy (A:).

Click Save.

Open the folder where the document(s) to be saved on to floppy are located.

Select document(s). If more than one, hold CTRL key down and select as desired.

Right-click on blue documents, slide down to Send to, across to 3½ Floppy, and left-click.

FOLDER, NEW

Click My Computer—the computer screen icon on the bottom taskbar.

Browse through the C drive to folder to where you want the new folder to go.

Get File menu and slide down to New.

Across to Folder and single left-click.

Name folder and hit Enter.

FONT SIZE—CHANGING TO DEFAULT

Open a file.

Select text to be changed.

Change to different font and size by going to the tool bar clicking on the arrow next to size or font. Reach the desired "look" and save and all future text will appear as selected.

See also: SELECTING

Fs ON KEYBOARD (when using Word program)

F1   Help—also same as top bar Help.

F5   Does the work of Find, Replace, Go to. *Note*: If you select a part of the article you can then use copy/paste.

F7   Spelling/grammar.

GAME, FREE CELL—TO PLAY

Click Start, All Programs, Games, Free Cell

Click Game, New Game

GLITCHES—ON EXPLORER OR ON ANY PROGRAM
Press Ctrl + Alt and hold both down. Tap Delete. Brings up Task Manager.
Box shows all programs.
Make sure you are in Applications tab.
On blue bar may appear "Not Responding". If so, click End task (bottom left of box).

HEADINGS
Click on the word you want to make into a heading.
Click on Style box, top left three or four bars down, and click on arrow.
On menu, click on required type.

HIGHLIGHTING
You can use Shift + arrows to locate desired spot more accurately and easily.

HIGHLIGHTING TEXT IN A WORD DOCUMENT
The **A** icon on top bar changes the color of the type.
The Highlighter icon (small square + highlighter pen) puts bright highlight color over the words.
Select area to color with cursor.
Select color.

HYPERLINKS
Hyperlinks are anything that lights up on screen for you to click. Select the hyperlink, then left-click or Ctrl + left click and underline. This takes you directly to Web site or e-mail. Compose.

ICONS—CHANGING (any: Desktop; Internet, etc.)
This applies to icons on folders.
Right-click on icon.
Get Properties. Click on Customize, then click on:
Change icon. Go to Change icon at bottom of Box.

Then:
Click on one you want.
Click OK.
Click Apply, then OK in next box.

INSERTING FILES INTO A WORD DOCUMENT
For example, if you wanted to insert a piece of poetry into your book chapter.
Open document where you want the other document to go.
Left-click Insert, File.
Browse folders for file to be inserted and double left-click the file name in the list.

INSERTING SYMBOLS (in Word program)
Symbol is a useful function for all sorts of signs, symbols, etc. Click cursor where you want symbol. Go to Insert then Symbol, click Insert, click Close. You can also use Autoshapes on top bar, but it is quicker to go to Symbols on the Insert menu on top bar.
Also useful are Page numbers, Picture, Bookmark.
Note: instead of Insert/Picture/Autoshapes, go direct to middle bar and click Autoshapes. Best for arrows, etc.

INTERNET—SAVING A PAGE OR PICTURE
Right-click on picture or writing.
Click Save picture as. Save into desired folder.

LETTER, NEW—OPENING UP
There are two icons on bottom bar.
A **W** in a square icon for blank paper.
A star in a square box for letterhead paper.

LINE SPACING (in Word program)
Select text.
Go Format (top bar), then Paragraph. Make adjustment.
or Select text, click Line spacing button on one of the top toolbars and change there.

MESSAGE—ATTACHMENT (PICTURE OR WHATEVER)
Open new e-mail.
Click Insert, then File Attachment.
Browse for document.
Double left-click.
Do addresses and message text.
Click Send.

MOVING WORDS OR PHRASES OR PARAGRAPH
Select the word by using the cursor. Let go. Left-click and drag carefully. Text moves to where vertical bar appears.
or Select text, cut or copy, paste.

MOVE WRITING FROM ONE WORD DOCUMENT TO ANOTHER
Open document you wish to move writing from.
Open document you wish to move writing to.
You will have two documents listed down on the bottom on the taskbar.
Click the "From" document to bring it to the front.
Highlight the text you wish to move, then either copy or cut it from document.
Click the "To" document to bring it to the front.
Place cursor where you want the text to go in the document.
Paste the text in.
Save changes as desired in both To and From documents.

MUSIC
If there is music already in hard drive:
Open Windows Media Player icon (square with circle inside and cross wires plus arrow).
Click Media Library.
Find music in playlist.
Double left-click track.
To enter new music:

Put CD into hard drive. Wait. It starts automatically in Windows Media Player.
Press Copy from CD button on left.
Press Copy music (up top).
Press Media Library button left.
Select all the songs.
Right click, down to Add to Playlist, left-click.
Double-click the Playlist where you want the songs to go OR create a NEW Playlist by clicking the NEW button, typing a name, and clicking OK.

NUMBERING—PAGES, ETC. IN WORD
Go to Insert on top bar, left-click.
Menu—click Page numbers.
Box—choose position: top left, top right, whatever. Choose format.

PAGES, USING SCROLL BUTTON
Having opened up a longer document, to go to a certain page left click on scroll button on right side of screen and hold and move up and down. A menu appears when you left click, next to the button, showing "Top heading" and also which page you are looking at. (Also, there are buttons at the bottom left of screen above Start. If you left-click on these four buttons you get a response. The second from left orders Print Layout View—the most useful.
Also: Left-click on page. Tap scroll wheel on mouse. Sign appears (arrow up, arrow down, plus tiny circle in between). You can push mouse up and down to scroll instead of rolling the wheel.

PARAGRAPHS—NUMBERING
Complete typing. Place cursor at start of the paragraph to be numbered, highlight the entire paragraph. Click on paragraph numbering icon on bar. Paragraph numbering must be continuous.
or Click "Bullets" instead.

PROGRAMS—ADD/REMOVE
Left-click Start.
Left-click Control Panel.
Double left-click Add/Remove Programs.
Find program to be removed.
Click on program to be removed. It goes blue.
Click on Change/Remove.
Click Yes and then OK or Finish.

RE-BOOTING
Close all programs.
Go to Start, then Turn Off Computer, then Restart.

RECYCLE BIN—EMPTYING
On desktop, right-click on Recycle Bin icon.
On next box, click on Empty Recycle Bin.
Click Yes.

RECYCLE BIN—RESTORING FROM
Double left-click on recycle bin icon on desktop.
Left-click file and click on Restore.

SAVE and SAVE AS—DIFFERENCES BETWEEN
"Save" is used when you have a document that has already been named.
"Save as" is used when you first open a document *or* when you want to alter a draft document of any sort *or* to make a second document.

SAVE—HOW TO DO IT—3 WAYS in WORD
Use top bar and click on the "TV" icon.
Use CTRL + S.
Go to File and then on menu Save.

SAVE AS—HOW TO DO IT
Write the article, or part of it.
Click on File.
Click on Save as.
Make sure Save in is where you actually want to save it,

i.e., in the proper folder. To do that, click on downward-pointing arrow to right of Save in box.
Browse through directory until you get the folder you want.
Type in file name and then click Save.

SCREEN VIEW IN WORD
Remember the four boxes, bottom left: Normal, Web, Print, Outline.

SELECTING—WHEN DEALING WITH TEXT
Works with either Copy, Delete, Bold, Center.
Place cursor at start of script to be selected and drag.
or Once cursor is in place, use Shift key + the four arrow keys.
or Double click to select a word;
or Triple click to select a paragraph.
or Click, hold and drag.

SPACING BETWEEN LINES
See LINE, SPACING

SYMBOLS, INSERTING
See INSERTING SYMBOLS

TIME—SETTING
Double click the time in the bottom right hand corner.
Make changes and click OK.

TITLE—CHANGING/RENAMING
Open folder where document is stored.
Slowly, left-click twice on the title. Box appears with blue color.
Click where you want to make a change on the title.
After altering, left-click anywhere or press Enter.

VOLUME BUTTON FOR SOUND
Click on Loudspeaker icon, bottom right-hand corner.
Use menu to adjust sound volume.

WORD—ERRORS
May get green squiggly line, which means error in grammar, so right-click cursor on the word or phrase and see what the program says. Chose the Ignore or Accept bar. A red squiggly line is a spelling error. Right-click on the word and choose option.

WORDS—COUNTING NUMBER OF
To obtain number of words, characters, paragraphs, pages, and lines:
Click Tools, go to Word Count and click.

WRITINGS—STORED—DELETING
Find document in folder:
Method A: Left- or right-click. Drag to Recycle icon on desktop.
Method B: Right-click on document name. Left-click on Delete.
Method C: Click on file to be deleted. Hit Del on keyboard.
If more than one document, click on one and hold down CTRL at same time. Then click on others to be deleted. Then use one of the three methods to delete.

WRITINGS—STORED—FINDING
Click Start, Search.
Get Search Results box.
Click All Files and Folders.
Type in on named bar the name of file.
Click Search.
Note: Use Maximize on bar to make reading easier. Scroll to ensure you view all documents. Useful if you cannot recall where you stored the file.

WWW—COPYING TEXT FROM WEB PAGE TO WORD DOCUMENT
Open Internet Explorer browser—e symbol on bottom taskbar.

Page defaults to Google search engine, which is the best one. If is doesn't type *www.google.com*.

Type query in Google search box in middle of page—*not* up in the top address box.

For example—"talked the sun down from the sky" if it is a direct quote or *outward bound Australia* if it is a general query.

Hit Search or Enter and wait for search results.

You then have a look at the results by clicking the blue link to find one that looks like it will give you the info you want. If you go to a page and it doesn't have the info required, hit the Back button up at the top of the browser page to go back to Google results and try another link.

When you find what you are looking for, you can then copy the text off the page by highlighting the desired text and copying it, using CTRL + C.

Then open a blank Word document and paste what you have copied, using CTRL + V.

Then go to File, Save as, browse to the desired storage folder, name the document, and hit Enter or Save.

Where You Can Go to Get Instruction

You can get computer training at a community college, and even some high schools offer courses designed specifically for seniors. The following schools provide training:

- New Horizons Computer Learning Center
- ITT Technical Institute
- Westwood College of Technology
- Boston University Corporate Education Center
- University of Phoenix

All have technology programs, some of which may be convenient for you. To access a more complete list, which includes many local locations, have a friend who is computer literate go to: *http://www.computertrainingschools.com/featured/search.php* and print out the appropriate locations for you.

Some have found it easier to contact a high school or college student who is a neighbor and pay them to teach the fundamentals. Of course, these kids are not professional instructors, but you can inexpensively get the basics from any youngster. They are all Internet literate, so choose one the way you would choose a babysitter: someone with good communications skills and someone you like and trust.

Internet access provider EarthLink has a program called Generation-Link that matches high school students with older adults interested in learning the computer, and SeniorNet and CyberSeniors are two organizations that also provide training.

Learn How to Use the Internet/Find Information Online

A course from Learn The Net, a privately held company based in San Francisco, California, focuses on delivering high-quality educational products and services in print, CD-ROM, and to the desktop, via the Internet and intranets. The cost is $6.95, and the course lasts one hour.

> Course Description: With hundreds of millions of pages, you could spend a lifetime surfing the World Wide Web, following links from one place to another. Amusing, perhaps, but not very productive. One of the biggest problems with the Web is finding specific information. Where do you start? By learning how to use Web-based search tools you can quickly find up-to-date, reliable information.

At the end of this course, you will be able to:
- Effectively manage search functions on the Web.
- Understand the categorization of information in different search engines.
- Use Yahoo! and AltaVista.
- Perform metasearches.
- Refine search queries to target information.
- Evaluate online information.

BECOME COMPUTER LITERATE

Prerequisites : None
System Requirements : Internet Access

You must have access to a computer and go to their site *http://www.learnthenet.com/*.

AARP offers help in learning how to use the Internet. This tutorial is for intermediate users, people who already have some familiarity with the Net. Go to *http://www.aarp.org/learnInternet/*.

Books You Can Purchase

If you do not have access to a computer, you can start the process of learning how to use the Internet by purchasing *Internet for Dummies* by John R. Levine, Carol Baroudi, and Margaret Levine Young. Here is what Amazon.com says about this book: "Even if you're not a dummy, the sixth edition of *The Internet for Dummies* is one of the best user's guides to the Internet now available. Many so-called Internet books are nothing more than printed collections of Web addresses."

Many other books can also help, including *The Complete Idiot's Guide to PCs* (8th edition) by Joe Kraynak, *Internet Explorer 6 for Dummies* by Doug Lowe, and *PCs for Dummies* (5th edition) by Dan Gookin, to name a few.

You can also get Internet instructions from DVDs sold through Amazon or major bookstores everywhere.

You will have to eventually use a computer with Internet access to practice what you have learned. Remember, this is easy, *and* you can always get help from your grandchildren.

Protect Your Good Credit

Chapter Overview

- Design a Budget
- Identity Fraud
- If You Are a Victim
- "Do Not Call" Registry
- Check Your Credit Regularly/Free Credit Reports
- Invest in a Shredder

Everybody knows that protecting their credit from identify fraud has become an important part of life. Below I've included information to help you do so. According to a recent study by the Federal Reserve, almost 80 percent of seniors have credit scores of 701 or better, and another 10 percent have scores of 660 to 700. These high scores should qualify most seniors for the lowest interest rates. If you can qualify for a lower interest rate that you are currently getting, by all means do so. Of course, credit thieves target seniors as they know their credit is usually excellent.

Design a Budget

Most experts suggest that seniors should design a reasonable monthly budget that they are comfortable with and that does not strain their resources. You should track your expenses as they are incurred and make sure you are not spending more than you have budgeted.

Identity Fraud

You must also protect yourself against people stealing your identity and against fraud. Never give personal information to someone you don't know and trust. This is especially true of your Social Security number, date of birth, bank account number, credit card numbers, and home address. *Do not keep your Social Security number in your purse or wallet*, and carry as little identifying information as possible. Make a photocopy of what you do carry with you and keep it in a safe place that you can refer to in case your purse or wallet is stolen or misplaced.

One of the most common scams is for a bogus credit card company to ask you to pay upfront to get approved for their credit card. Legitimate credit card companies don't require upfront payment. Also remember that if a deal sounds too good to be true, it usually is. You can verify the legitimacy of offers you receive with your local Better Business Bureau at *http://www.bbb.org/*.

If You Are a Victim
If you have been scammed or are a victim of credit card fraud, notify all credit card companies and tell them to issue you a new card; contact the three major credit bureaus and request that they put a fraud alert on your credit report. The companies and their contact numbers are Equifax, 800-525-6285; Experian, 888-397-3742; and TransUnion, 800-680-7289.

You should also contact your local law enforcement agency. Complaints can be filed as well by calling 877-IDTHEFT or logging on to the FTC Web site at *http://www.consumer.gov/idtheft/*.

"Do Not Call" Registry
Seniors are the group of Americans that are most likely to be scammed. To cut down the likelihood of becoming a victim, sign up with the National Do Not Call Registry by calling 1-888-382-1222 or go online to *http://www.donotcall.gov*. Signing up with the registry will remove your name from most direct marketing company lists. If you are contacted by phone or by e-mail, remember that most offers that sound to good to be true are. Another word of advice: do not pay up-front handling fees or advanced fees for services; ask for everything in writing, and never give out your credit card number to unknown parties that are soliciting you by phone or via the Internet.

Check Your Credit Regularly/ Free Credit Reports
Monitoring your own credit report is an excellent way to protect yourself against identify theft. A law was passed in 2003 that makes everyone in the United States eligible to order a free credit report once a year from each of the three major credit reporting agencies. You can order all three reports at once, or a report every three months or so within the year from Equifax, Experian, and Trans Union.

Do not contact the three nationwide consumer reporting companies individually. They are only providing free annual credit reports through *www.annualcreditreport.com* or by calling toll free, 877-322-8228. To order by mail go to *www.annualcreditreport.com* and print out the form, fill it out, and send it to Annual Credit Report Request Service, P.O. Box 105281, Atlanta, GA 30348-5281.

If you wish to get more information, go to the Federal Trade Commission's Web site, *www.ftc.gov*.

See Appendix 6 for a list of common scams.

Invest in a Shredder

Consider investing in a shredder. They are not expensive, and if you shred all documents that have your personal information on them as well as all credit card and other mailings that solicit you for new cards, you will keep credit thieves from obtaining this information from your trash. Shredders can be purchased at office supply stores as well as at Costco, Wal-Mart, Target, and other superstores.

Health Insurance Costs

Chapter Overview

- Planning for Increases
- Health Savings Accounts
- Medicare Supplement Insurance
- COBRA

Retirees and seniors thinking about retiring must plan for health-care costs, or they will likely find themselves facing financial problems. As one gets older health care becomes more expensive. A study by the Institute for the Future found that seven in ten Medicare beneficiaries have two or more chronic ailments and that roughly half of Americans now turning 65 will at some point spend time in a nursing home, with one in ten staying three years or longer. The federal Centers for Medicare & Medicaid Services performed a 2004 study which found that health-care spending in the United States surged to $1.6 trillion in 2002. Prescription drug costs grew 15.3 percent for the year, far outstripping the growth of most pension checks and Social Security checks. According to the Kaiser Family Foundation and the Health Research & Educational Trust, family premiums in 2004 in employer-sponsored health-care plans rose 11.2 percent over the previous year to $9,950.

Planning for Increases

Why provide you with all these scary numbers? In order to make sure you understand that although Medicare helps, it will not entirely solve the problem of high health-care costs. You must plan for it yourself. Take a good look at how much you'll need for health-care costs. If you have not retired yet, consider postponing retirement a bit if you can't find ways to cover the costs. If you have already retired, consider taking a part-time or temporary job or reducing your month-to-month expenses accordingly. This advice is particularly important for seniors hoping to retire before Medicare coverage takes place.

Employers are finding that paying health benefits to their retirees is becoming so expensive that they are looking for ways to cut these expenses. Seventy-nine percent of employers in 2004 raised the portion of the premium they expect retirees to pay, said Alix Nyberg in the February 2005 issue of *CFO Magazine*.

According to a Kaiser/Hewitt 2004 survey of companies with one thousand or more employees:

- 85 percent will very likely or likely increase retiree contribution to premiums for health benefits
- 51 percent will very likely or likely increase retiree co-insurance or co-pay
- 49 percent will very likely or likely increase retiree drug co-insurance or co-pay

With this information in mind, seniors should be planning to pay for a larger portion of their health insurance in the coming years. The costs for health insurance prior to reaching the age of 65 when Medicare becomes available are substantial. Depending on the policy it can be thousands of dollars a year.

Health Savings Accounts

Health savings accounts or HSAs that became available via the 2003 Medicare Drug Act are a way to help pay for these costs. They allow employees to save up to $2,650 on a pretax basis per year for future medical care. These are employee-owned accounts that can be moved if you change employer. All funds that accumulate in these accounts are tax free.

Some employers provide employees nearing retirement with health reimbursement arrangements, which allow employers to credit amounts of money toward a retiree's medical benefits. These accounts can't be used prior to retirement. Ask your employer if such a plan is available for you.

Medicare Supplement Insurance

Once you reach 65 a Medicare supplement insurance policy can be purchased for comparatively little money. Some of these policies include partial payment for prescription drugs. In order to be eligible for any kind of health insurance that does not exclude preexisting conditions, you must present a certificate of creditable coverage to the insuring company.

This document will show that you had insurance prior to switching coverage. If you are unable to secure this document, any condition you had prior to your new insurance becoming in force will not be covered. Thus, it is very important that you maintain your old insurance while applying for new coverage.

COBRA

If you leave your current job you can COBRA (Consolidated Omnibus Budget Reconciliation Act) their insurance for a year and a half. Under COBRA, you must pay the full costs of the insurance yourself, but at the rate your employer is currently paying for your coverage. COBRA applies to both employee and family if the family has had prior coverage.

For more information on COBRA go to the U.S. Department of Labor Web site, *http://www.dol.gov/dol/topic/health-plans/cobra.htm*.

According to the Labor Department, "The Consolidated Omnibus Budget Reconciliation Act (COBRA) gives workers and their families who lose their health benefits the right to choose to continue group health benefits provided by their group health plan for limited periods of time under certain circumstances such as voluntary or involuntary job loss, reduction in the hours worked, transition between jobs, death, divorce, and other life events. Qualified individuals may be required to pay the entire premium for coverage up to 102 percent of the cost to the plan."

COBRA generally requires that group health plans sponsored by employers with twenty or more employees in the prior year offer employees and their families the opportunity for a temporary extension of health coverage (called continuation coverage) in certain instances where coverage under the plan would otherwise end.

COBRA outlines how employees and family members may elect continuation coverage. It also requires employers and plans to provide notice.

Prescription Drugs

Chapter Overview

- Medicare Prescription Drug Plan
- Medicare Part D Questions to Consider
- Deducting Medical Expenses from Your Income Tax
- Keeping Track of Your Prescriptions
- Tips for Saving on Prescription Drugs
- Is Buying Prescription Drugs Online Safe?
- Should I Consider Purchasing Canadian Drugs?
- Consumer Tips
- To Start Your Search
- Buy Online
- Other Health Issues

Most seniors find that prescription drugs are not covered by their insurance. Information on Medicare-approved prescription drug cards and Medicare Part D can be found on *http://www.Medicare.gov*. What is covered, what will be covered, and how it will be covered are changing, and the easiest way to keep up with what is happening now is to go to the Medicare and Medicaid sites for up-to-date information.

You can also visit *http://www.aarp.org/health/medicare/drug_coverage/* to check out the new Guide to Medicare Prescription Drug Coverage, and how the Medicare drug benefits work with other coverage. This free guide will help you choose from many private plans approved by Medicare, and give you information on the cost and benefits as well as whether you qualify for extra help. The plan currently will have an open enrollment period each November allowing you to enroll or switch plans. It is also necessary to enroll when you are first eligible for Medicare, or your monthly premiums are likely to be higher.

AARP sometimes changes its links, so if you can't get to this area using the link above, go to *http://www.aarp.org/* and click on Health.

New legislation is constantly being enacted, and prescription drug coverage will change from time to time. AARP provides up-to-date information on its Web site. If you are not computer literate it would be worthwhile for you to ask a friend or perhaps one of your children or grandchildren to print out this information for you so you can order this free guide.

Medicare Prescription Drug Plan

This plan provides Medicare-eligible seniors the opportunity to enroll in a Medicare-approved prescription insurance plan. ***Important: check enrollment dates as they change as the plan goes forward.***

To be eligible you must be 65 years or older and eligible to receive Social Security or under 65, permanently disabled

PRESCRIPTION DRUGS 95

and have received Social Security disability insurance payments for at least two years. Patients who have been receiving continuing dialysis for permanent kidney failure or need a kidney transplant or have (ALS/Lou Gehrig's disease) are also eligible.

The various Medicare 2006 prescription drug plans will offer, for those who qualify, conventional prescription drug coverage similar to other prescription insurance plans, where an enrollee pays a monthly premium and a co-pay or coinsurance for each prescription they fill.

If you have state Medicaid prescription drug coverage you will automatically be enrolled in a Medicare prescription plan.

Go to the Medicare site: *http://www.medicare.gov/pdp home.asp* to find out more details about this plan. *The information below will change as time progresses so it is necessary to either go to the Medicare site or check with your insurance professional to keep updated on changes.*

Areas the Medicare site covers include:

What is Medicare prescription drug coverage?
Medicare prescription drug coverage is insurance that covers both brand-name and generic prescription drugs at participating pharmacies in your area. Medicare prescription drug coverage provides protection for people who have very high drug costs.

Who can get Medicare prescription drug coverage?
Everyone with Medicare is eligible for this coverage, regardless of income and resources, health status, or current prescription expenses.

When can I get Medicare prescription drug coverage?
You may sign up by May 15, 2006. If you don't sign up when you are first eligible or by May 15, 2006, you may pay a penalty. Your next opportunity to enroll is from November 15, 2006, to December 31, 2006.

How does Medicare prescription drug coverage work?
Your decision about Medicare prescription drug coverage depends on the kind of health-care coverage you have now. There are two ways to get Medicare prescription drug coverage. You can join a Medicare prescription drug plan or you can join a Medicare Advantage Plan or other Medicare Health Plans that offer drug coverage.

Whatever plan you choose, Medicare drug coverage will help you by covering brand-name and generic drugs at pharmacies that are convenient for you.

Like other insurance, if you join, you will pay a monthly premium, which varies by plan, and a yearly deductible (no more than $250 in 2006). You will also pay a part of the cost of your prescriptions, including a co-payment or coinsurance. Costs will vary depending on which drug plan you choose. Some plans may offer more coverage and additional drugs for a higher monthly premium. If you have limited income and resources, and you qualify for extra help, you may not have to pay a premium or deductible.

Why should I get Medicare prescription drug coverage?
Medicare prescription drug coverage provides greater peace of mind by protecting you from unexpected drug expenses. Even if you don't use a lot of prescription drugs now, you should still consider joining. As we age, most people need prescription drugs to stay healthy. For most people, joining now means protecting yourself from unexpected prescription drug bills in the future.

What if I have a limited income and resources?
There is extra help for people with limited income and resources. Almost one in three people with Medicare will qualify for extra help, and Medicare will pay for almost all of their prescription drug costs.

Things to Consider
To get Medicare coverage for your prescription drugs, you must choose and join a Medicare drug plan. Regardless of

PRESCRIPTION DRUGS 97

how a Medicare drug plan decides to offer this coverage, there are some key factors that may vary. Some of these factors might be more important to you than others, depending on your situation and drug needs. These factors are:
- Cost
- Coverage
- Convenience
- Peace of mind now and in the future

Cost

Premium
This is the monthly cost you pay to join a Medicare drug plan. Premiums vary by plan.

Deductible
This is the amount you pay for your prescriptions before your plan starts to share in the costs. Deductibles vary by plans. No plan may have a deductible more than $250 in 2006.

Copayment/Coinsurance
This is the amount you pay for your prescriptions after you have paid the deductible. In some plans, you pay the same copayment (a set amount) or coinsurance (a percentage of the cost) for any prescription. In other plans, there might be different levels or "tiers," with different costs. (For example, you might have to pay less for generic drugs than brand names. Or some brand names might have a lower copayment than other brand names.) Also, in some plans your share of the cost can increase when your prescription drug costs reach a certain limit.

Coverage

Formulary
A list of drugs that a Medicare drug plan covers is called a formulary. Formularies include generic drugs and brand-name drugs. Most prescription drugs used by people with

Medicare will be on a plan's formulary. The formulary must include at least two drugs in categories and classes of most commonly prescribed drugs to people with Medicare. This makes sure that people with different medical conditions can get the treatment they need.

Prior Authorization
Some drugs are more expensive than others even though some less expensive drugs work just as well. Other drugs may have more side effects, or have restrictions on how long they can be taken. To be sure certain drugs are used correctly and only when truly necessary, plans may require a "prior authorization." This means before the plan will cover these prescriptions, your doctor must first contact the plan and show there is a medically necessary reason you must use that particular drug for it to be covered. Plans might have other rules like this to ensure that your drug use is effective.

Coverage Gap
If you have high drug costs, you may consider which plans offer additional coverage until you spend $3,600 out-of-pocket. In some plans, if your costs reach an initial coverage limit, then you pay 100% of your prescription costs. This is called the coverage gap. This "gap" in coverage is generally above $2,250 in total drug costs until you spend $3,600 out-of-pocket. Some plans might offer some coverage during the gap. Even in plans where you pay 100% of covered drug costs after a certain limit, you would still pay less for your prescriptions than you would without this drug coverage.

Convenience
Drug plans must contract with pharmacies in your area. Check with the plan to make sure your pharmacy or a pharmacy in the plan is convenient to you. Also, some plans may offer a mail-order program that will allow you to have drugs sent directly to your home. You should consider all of your options in determining what is the most cost-effective and convenient way to have your prescriptions filled.

Prescription Drugs

Now and in the Future

Even if you don't take a lot of prescription drugs now, you still should consider joining a drug plan in 2006. As we age, most people need prescription drugs to stay healthy. For most people, joining now means you will pay a lower monthly premium in the future since you may have to pay a penalty if you choose to join later. You will have to pay this penalty as long as you have a Medicare drug plan. If you reach the point where you have spent $3,600 out-of-pocket for drug costs during the year, the plan will pay most of your remaining drug costs. This protection could start even sooner in some plans.

The following list of questions covers some common situations:

> "I have Original Medicare only, or Original Medicare and a Medigap ('Supplement') Policy without drug coverage."

If you use an average amount of prescription drugs, Medicare's new prescription drug coverage could pay over half of your drug costs next year. If you have very high unexpected drug costs, Medicare will pay up to 95% of these costs after you spend $3,600 out-of-pocket in a year.

What you need to do:

To get this drug coverage, you can join a Medicare Prescription Drug Plan that covers prescription drugs only and keep your Original Medicare coverage the way it is. Or you can join a Medicare Advantage Plan or other Medicare Health Plan that covers doctor and hospital care as well as prescriptions.

Medicare Advantage Plans usually give you extra benefits and/or lower costs, but only if you use the doctors and hospitals that participate in the plan's "network." If you do not opt for prescription drug coverage by May 15, 2006, you will have to pay a late enrollment penalty to get drug coverage later.

"I have Original Medicare and a Medigap ('Supplement') Policy with drug coverage."

Medicare prescription drug coverage will generally provide significant savings compared to what you are paying in copayments for drugs under your Medigap plan, and will generally provide much better protection against unexpected drug expenses as well.

What you need to do:
Decide between keeping your Medigap policy with drug coverage or joining a Medicare plan that offers prescription coverage. You have probably received information in the mail for plans in your area offering coverage. Compare your current coverage to the new Medicare coverage.

Unlike Medigap, most of the cost of Medicare drug coverage is paid by Medicare, and will never run out if you have unexpected drug costs. Also, if you do not join a Medicare Drug Plan or a Medicare Advantage Plan that offers prescription drug coverage by May 15, 2006, you will have to pay a late enrollment penalty to get drug coverage later. If you opt for Medicare prescription drug coverage, tell your insurer, and the drug portion of your Medigap policy will be removed.

"I am a retiree and I have drug coverage through my (or my spouse's) former employer or union."

Medicare will help employers or unions continue to provide retiree drug coverage that meets Medicare's standard. Your former employer or union has choices about how they will work with Medicare.

What you need to do:
Your former employer or union probably mailed you a letter already. This information will explain how they will work with Medicare on prescription drug coverage

Prescription Drugs

and what decisions you will have to make. If you do not hear from them, visit their website or call your benefits administrator.

"I have a Medicare Advantage Plan (like an HMO or PPO) or other Medicare Health Plan."

Medicare is working with Medicare Advantage and other Medicare Health Plans to help them provide even more coverage and/or lower costs. Your plan will let you know about the prescription drug options they will offer. You can also choose to switch to another Medicare Advantage Plan or Medicare Health Plan. Or you could choose the Original Medicare Plan and join a Medicare Prescription Drug Plan.

What you need to do:
Read the information you got in the mail explaining any additional prescription drug coverage your plan will offer.

"I have Medicare and Medicaid, and I get my drug coverage from Medicaid."

Starting January 1, 2006, you will get your prescription drug coverage from Medicare instead of Medicaid. The prescription drug coverage from Medicare has no premiums, no deductibles, and no gaps, and you will pay very little or nothing for almost all prescriptions.

What you need to do:
Starting in the fall, you will need to decide which Medicare plan that offers prescription drug coverage you would like. If you do not sign up for a plan, Medicare will sign you up for one to make sure you do not miss a day of coverage. Medicare will send you a letter to let you know which plan you are in. You can switch to a different plan if you choose.

"I have limited resources and live on limited income."

What you need to do:

If your resources are less than $11,500 (single) or $23,000 (married), you may qualify for extra help paying for Medicare Prescription Drug Coverage. If you haven't received an application or information about the extra help, and you think you may be eligible, you should apply. Remember, as Department of Health and Human Services Secretary Leavitt says, "If in doubt, fill it out!" You can apply online by visiting the Help with Medicare Prescription Drug Plan Costs section on the *Social Security Administration Web site*.

Cost Estimator

Private companies will offer Medicare prescription drug coverage starting January 1, 2006. The decisions you make depend on what kind of health-care coverage you have now. To find out more about what Medicare drug coverage means to you, read our publication, *A Guide to Getting Started*.

Key factors to consider in comparing your drug plan options are: Coverage, cost, convenience, and peace of mind now and in the future. To find out more about these factors, read *Things to Think About When You Compare Plans*.

The cost estimator assumes that you have no current drug coverage or receive any type of discounts, such as from a drug discount card, on your prescription drug cost. If you know what you spend monthly on prescription drugs you can use the cost estimator to see what your potential savings will be by joining a Medicare prescription drug plan. It will also provide you with information on the lowest premium available in your state.

The cost estimator is a quick tool to give you a sense of the savings you can anticipate with Medicare Prescription Drug coverage. This tool is not able to take into account any insurance you may have now for drugs. Therefore, if you currently have insurance for drugs, the tool will not be able

Prescription Drugs

to compare current costs to those you may have in the future if you switch to Medicare drug coverage. If you would like more information on how the cost estimates are calculated, click here. *(Go to the Medicare site)*

Landscape of Local Plans
The Landscape of Local Plans lists all plans available in your area, providing important information on:

- Cost (premiums, deductibles and payments)
- Coverage (important issues around what and how drugs are covered)
- Convenience (pharmacy and mail-order options)

For more tips on how to use the Landscape, see *Answers to Key Questions.*

The Landscape provides information about the two different ways you can get your Medicare drug coverage:

- Stand-alone Prescription Drug Plans that offer drug coverage only. You can add drug coverage to the Original Medicare plan and some Medicare Advantage and other Medicare Health Plans through a "stand alone" prescription drug plan (PDP). To learn more about how to read Stand-alone Prescription Drug Plans Landscape, click here. *(Go to the Medicare site)*
- Medicare Advantage or other Health Plans with Prescription Drug Coverage. Or, you can get drug coverage and the rest of your Medicare coverage through a Medicare Advantage (MA) or other health plan, like an HMO or PPO, which typically provides more benefits at a significantly lower cost through a network of doctors and hospitals. [Please note, a dash in the "Beneficiary Drug Premium" column means that plan does not offer prescription drug coverage.] To learn more about how to read the Medicare Advantage, Cost Plans, and Demonstrations Landscape,

Medicare Prescription Drug Plan Finder
Starting January 1, 2006, new Medicare prescription drug coverage will be available to everyone with Medicare, regardless of income, health status, or how you pay for prescription drugs today.

Everyone with Medicare needs to make a decision about prescription drug coverage. Even if you don't use a lot of prescription drugs now, you should still consider joining a plan. **Remember, to get the coverage, you must join a plan.**

The Medicare Prescription Drug Plan Finder will help you:

- Learn about the new Medicare prescription drug coverage.
- Find and compare prescription drug plans that meet your personal needs.
- Enroll in the prescription drug plan that you select.

Medicare Prescription Drug Plan Finder—Online Demo
This Flash movie demo walks you through the new Medicare Prescription Drug Plan Finder. *(Go to the Medicare site)*

Formulary (Drug) Finder
Lets you enter the drugs you use to find out which plans in an area have formularies that cover these drugs. *(Go to the Medicare site)*

Medicare Part D Questions to Consider

- How much am I paying for my prescription drugs now?
- Will these prescriptions be covered under the Part D prescription drug benefit, and will there be a deductible?
- Will there be a premium that I have to pay to get this coverage, and if so, how much?
- When must I sign up for one of these programs, and what happens if I don't sign up within the prescribed time?

For information on Medicaid go to *http://cms.hhs.gov.* and click on Medicare Prescription Drug Coverage. You can also click on Medicaid under the Programs listing. This most useful site also has a complete alphabetical list of topics related to Medicaid. Anything you want to know is likely to be on this list, and it is updated regularly. To reach this list click on Medicaid Index (a topical listing of Medicaid subject areas).

Those who are not computer literate and don't have someone to help get this information from the Medicare and Medicaid sites may call 1-800-Medicare. You may also get a copy of the page for professionals who assist older and disabled Americans with Medicare from the Medicare Rights Center, *http://www.medicarerights.org/* and click on Publications. This site also has a chart that will help you compare your Medicare options and has put together a list of discount drug programs. It contains eligibility and benefit information on state prescription drug assistance programs, drug discount cards, and Internet and mail-order discount pharmacies.

Deducting Medical Expenses from Your Income Tax

Check out IRS publication 502, *http://www.irs.gov/publications/p502/*.

Seniors can group all their medical expenses—including prescription drugs, diabetes meters, hearing aids, and so on—and if the total comes to more than 7.5 percent of their adjusted gross income, IRS allows for a deduction. Only expenses paid for during the year you are taking the deduction will apply, regardless of when you used the product or service. Medical expenses that have been reimbursed by insurance or Medicare cannot be included in the total.

Keep Track of Your Prescriptions

It is a good idea to make a list of all the prescription drugs you take, along with their respective dosages, and carry it with you. You should also show this list to your physicians so they all have a record and can look out for possible interactions with future drugs they may prescribe.

Tips for Savings on Prescription Drugs

1. Always ask your physician if there is a generic equivalent. The savings over brand-name drugs are often as much as 70 percent.
2. Check the costs of your prescriptions at several pharmacies as well as stores like Costco, Wal-Mart, and Target. Even different stores in the same chain have varying prices. After collecting this information go to your local or most convenient pharmacy and ask to speak to the owner or head pharmacist. Show the lower costs and ask if they can be met.
3. Ask your physician to prescribe a larger dosage of prescriptions that can be split (some can and some can't). Buy a pill splitter and cut the pill in half. Often the cost of a higher dosage is only slightly more than a dosage of one-half the milligrams. Some typical savings are 33 percent on Lipitor, 46 percent on Paxil, and 41 percent on Klonopin, according *U.S. News & World Report* research.
4. Purchase mail-order prescriptions from reputable mail-order pharmacies. You will often have to order three-month supplies, but the savings are usually worth it.
5. Purchase prescriptions from reliable, licensed Canadian pharmacies. There have not been any cases of bogus or unsafe drugs being shipped from licensed pharmacies in Canada, but you should follow these rules to help ensure your safety. (See "Should I Consider Purchasing Canadian Drugs" later in this chapter.)

If you just need to fill a prescription once in a while it might not be worth your time to search for the best price, but if you take a drug regularly there can be a substantial savings to purchase either online or from Canada.

Is Buying Prescription Drugs Online Safe?

Many online pharmacies are perfectly legitimate businesses, but purchasers of medications via the Internet must be cautious as some prescriptions sold in this manner could be unapproved, outdated, or illegal products. Usually there is no guarantee that you are dealing with a licensed pharmacist or physician. The General Accounting Office has reported that as many as a third of the so-called online "pharmacies" appear to have no safeguards to protect the consumer. You have no guarantee that the prescriptions you are receiving are what you ordered. These sites you reach could be in the United States, but they could also be offshore. Any online pharmacy that fills a prescription that has not been written by a physician is breaking the law.

The National Association of Boards of Pharmacy (NABP) has developed criteria to certify Internet pharmacies to its standards. The NABP requires a pharmacy to comply with the licensing and inspection requirements of the state in which it is located and each state to which it dispenses medications. Pharmacies that are approved can be easily identified by the Verified Internet Pharmacy Practice Site (VIPPS) seal displayed. You can view the VIPPS site at *http://www.nabp.net* to look for approved pharmacies.

The following four online pharmacies have received approval from the National Consumers League:

> *http://www.cvs.com/*
> *http://www.drugstore.com/*
> *http://www.medco.com/*
> *http://www.planetrx.com/*

Many seniors also purchase their scripts from *http://www.walgreens.com/*.

The publisher of *Consumer Reports* has launched a free Web site that gives information as to their rated "best buys" for prescription drugs and in some cases over-the-counter alternatives. Go to *http://www.consumerreports.org/* and click on Best Buy Drugs.

Get the Best Price

To compare prices for your prescriptions, simply click Compare prices for your prescriptions, then click on Quick search (one of the tabs at the top of the drug card page). Enter the name of a drug, and the site will give you generic lower-cost alternatives for many but not all brand-name medications.

Enter the name of drug (for example, Zocor) and click on Add drug. You are asked to enter the dosage and your ZIP code. After reviewing the user agreement you can click a tab that says More ways to save and then Compare options, and you will see a list of prices for a similar drug in the dosage you are taking. Of course, these prices are average prices across the United States, but you will have an excellent basis on which to judge comparative costs.

Contact Medicare by phone 1-800-MEDICARE (1-800-633-4227) to answer questions and to walk you through the process of how to save using the Medicare Web site.

The Medicare site also answers all kinds of questions. For example:

> **Question:** I've heard that I might be able to get a $600 credit to help pay for my prescription drugs. How does that work?
>
> **Answer:** If your annual gross income is below a certain level, Medicare may pay your annual enrollment fee for the Medicare-approved drug discount card and provide up to a $600 credit on your card each calendar year (2004 and 2005) toward your prescription drugs. You can use the $600 credit toward most prescriptions, even those not on the discount drug list. If you get the $600 credit to help you pay for your prescriptions, you

will still have to pay a percentage of the cost for each prescription.

This site also gives you excellent information on other assistance programs. You can identify Medicare-approved drug discount cards, their drug prices, and other programs that may assist with your prescription drug costs.

The National Council on Aging, *http://www.benefitscheck up.org/*, provides a tool called *BenefitsCheckUp* that helps you find programs for people ages 55 and over that may pay for some of the costs of prescription drugs, health care, utilities, and other essential items or services. *BenefitsCheckUpRX* assists with prescription drug savings. You will have to fill out a short confidential questionnaire in order to receive appropriate information. According to the National Council of Aging, millions of Americans are entitled to benefits that they are not receiving as they are not aware of their eligibility.

Companies like Caremark RX, Express Scripts, and Medco Health Solutions offer non-Medicare drug discount cards through both employers and insurers, and United in Minneapolis has issued a card and is partnering with AARP. United has still another card in a joint venture with Pfizer, Eli Lilly, and other pharmaceutical manufactures.

Small pharmacies sell about 44 percent of all prescription drugs in the United States, but times are changing. Larger chains like Walgreen's, with almost forty-five hundred stores, now offers its own card which is also good in an additional thirty-six thousand drugstore "partners" across the country. Each year there will be new offerings, and by 2008, according to Richard Evans of Sanford Bernstein, "The volume-price trade-off will be a wash for drug makers."

It is getting increasingly difficult for a senior to figure out which is the best or most cost-effective way to purchase prescription drugs. There are currently many ways to save, and this section covers only a few of them.

Should I Consider Purchasing Canadian Drugs?

The following information on buying drugs in Canada is taken from *http://www.oregon.gov/*:

> Over the past several years, an estimated 1 million US citizens [have been] traveling to Canada to buy cheaper prescription drugs. They are crossing the border in person, by telephone, by fax and over the Internet. Recent news coverage has many patients asking their doctors for advice about the safety of buying drugs in Canada—even if buying them is legal. Doctors often find themselves at a loss for answers.
>
> *Are these purchases legal?*
> The legal sands are shifting. The House and Senate have passed several different versions of legislation allowing drug imports, and the penalties for breaking the law are still unclear. The FDA has declined to prosecute persons involved in these transactions, but it is not as clear about cities and states that choose this option. The FDA will instead focus on the middlemen.
>
> *Are these purchases safe?*
> The drug approval process in Canada is similar to that followed in the US. Canada's pricing guidelines tether the price of new medications both to those of existing medications and to the other consumer goods. These guidelines have contributed to an increasing disparity between US and Canadian drug prices...that are on the average, 67 percent higher than the Canadian prices.
>
> *What are the mechanics of obtaining a prescription?*
> A valid prescription from a US physician is required, and often a patient's medical history is solicited as well. In the Canadian pharmacy participating in the

arrangement, the prescription is reissued by a Canadian physician and then filled by a Canadian pharmacist. Narcotics, benzodiazepines, and other drugs with the potential for abuse are generally not available.

What is the evidence of harm?
Evidence of harm from these transactions is sparse. However the possibility of harm may escalate in the future. Especially in the murky marketplace of the Internet, US consumers have no way of knowing with certainty the true origin of drugs ordered from Canadian sites.

Consumer Tips

- Don't buy from sites that offer to provide drugs that have not been approved by the FDA.
- Reputable online pharmacies will always ask for a prescription to be mailed or for a doctor's phone number to verify the order.
- Do not do business with sites that do not have a registered pharmacist who is available to answer your questions.
- Canadian law requires that prescriptions bear the signatures of Canadian physicians so check any script from Canada for a signature.
- Once the drugs arrive, compare the package and bills to the medication you already have at home. Check to make sure the expiration date is not less than three months away. An expiration date that is less than three months away is a red flag that the pharmacy may not be following traditional practices.
- Check for a street address and phone number when you are online. The site should also have a detailed privacy statement.
- Talk to your health-care professional before using any medications for the first time.

To Start Your Search

Check the exact names of your prescription drugs as well as the dosage prior to starting a price comparison search. Pricing varies substantially depending on dosage. Use the Internet to conduct your search. Medicare members who don't have access to the Internet can call 800-633-4227. Call Sunday and you are more likely to get through to Medicare more quickly. Compare Medicare drug card prices with deals offered through other sources, such as big discount stores. Stores like Costco, Target, or Internet discount pharmacies, such as *http://www.drugstore.com/*, often have better prices.

A report on prescription drugs prepared by Consumers Checkbook, a nonprofit consumer organization, is available free at *http://www.checkbook.org/*, where you can also get a guide with information on health care, top physicians, top dentists, top hospitals, health plans, etc.

If you are a good customer of a local pharmacy ask the owner, manager, or head pharmacist if they will meet a competitor's price; often they will do so.

The following sites offer good information with regard to prescription drugs:

- Price comparison tool: *http://www.medicare.gov/*. Type in your ZIP code and the drugs you take, and get information on which drug cards in your region offer the best prices and if the signup fee is worth it in your area.
- Medicare's guide to choosing a discount card: *www.medicare.gov/Publications*. You can also go to Medicare's Web site to help compare the different programs offered: *http://www.medicare.gov/AssistancePrograms*.

Buy Online

If you wish to purchase prescription drugs online and do not want to buy them from Canada, you can often save 20 percent to 50 percent off retail prices. To make sure the site is

Prescription Drugs

legitimate look for a Verified Internet Pharmacy Practice Site with a VIPPS seal. Remember to comparison shop for prescription drugs at the following Web sites: *http://www.pillbot.com/*, *http://www.pharmacychecker.com/*, and *http://corp.destinationrx.com/*.

Consult the following Web site for information about the medications you take:

- *http://www.safemedicines.org/issue.html*
- American Society of Health System Pharmacists: *http://www.ashp.org/*
- Food & Drug Administration's Consumer Drug Information: *http://www.fda.gov/cder/index.html*
- Search for information about drugs by name: *http://www.webmd.com/*
- National Library of Medicine: *http://www.medlineplus.gov/*
- Sharp Foundation, help identify pills by photos: *http://www.mypillbox.org/mypillbox.php*
- Updated information on the most prescribed drugs including side effects, drug interactions, dosage, and precautions: *http://www.rxlist.com/*
- Drug interaction checker, search function on twenty-four thousand drugs, drug news, and FDA actions: *http://www.cornellcares.com/*
- Drug alerts: *http://www.emedicine.com/*
- List of resources on new Medicare drug benefit: *http://kff.org/medicare/rxdrugdebate.cfm*

10

Assisted Living and Long-Term Care Insurance

Chapter Overview

- Housing Options for Seniors
- Home Health Care and Long-Term Care Insurance
- Choosing a Nursing Home
- Help from an Ombudsman

Providing for their own long-term care and assisted living is something most seniors don't like to think about, and consequently they often don't plan for it. It is also a subject that really should be discussed with your family so that plans can be made and options can be explored prior to the time such coverage become necessary.

Housing Options for Seniors

I cover briefly a number of options that are open to seniors. Costs will vary but they get considerably more expensive as you read down the list.

Of course, seniors or retirees can elect to live by themselves, but individuals or couples who choose to do so must be active and able to care for themselves. Home health aides are available to assist those in need of their services, and hospice workers can come into the home when a senior is in the last stage of life. Many seniors also arrange for live-in help which, although expensive, costs far less than most other choices.

Assisted living communities are designed for seniors who are having difficulty managing on their own, but who can provide a basic level of personal care including eating, taking their medication, and bathing without assistance.

Continuing care communities usually have facilities for seniors in various stages of the aging process. Many of these communities include independent housing, assisted living facilities, and nursing homes as well as rehabilitation care/facilities.

Nursing homes offer a higher level of medical care usually under the supervision of a physician and are designed for seniors who can't care for themselves, suffer from dementia or Alzheimer's, or are at the last stages of their lives.

A 2004 study by MetLife Mature Market Institute provides the following information: "The national average monthly cost for assisted living was $2,534. At the high end was Silver Spring, MD at $3,718 and at the lower end was $1,340 in Miami. The average cost to stay in a nursing home was

$192 per day. The average cost for home health aides was $18 per hour."

Home Health Care and Long-Term Care Insurance

Home health care and long-term care insurance pay for nursing home or health aides at home. The costs of these policies have risen substantially in the past few years. Check out several insurance companies prior to purchasing this kind of insurance and make sure to see if these carriers have raised their rates for existing customers over the past few years.

Make sure the insurer is a stable, reliable insurance company. There are rating services like *http://www.weissratings.com/*, *http://www.ambest.com/*, and *http://www2.standardandpoors.com/* that can help you do this.

- How long will this benefit be paid: one year, two years, five years? The length of coverage is one factor in determining the cost of the insurance.
- Check the benefit amount the insurance will pay you, such as $100, $150, or $200 per day. The amount of the benefit and the time that elapses between when you are medically certified to need it, your age at the time you purchase the insurance, and when the benefit actually begins have a great deal to do with determining the amount of your premium. It may take thirty to ninety days before receiving the first benefit payment after submitting a claim. Take this into consideration when choosing an "elimination period."

  One of the best ways to save on your premium is the purchase of a policy with a long elimination period. If the period is ninety days or even a year, the cost of the policy will be a great deal less than if the period is only thirty days or starts right away. However, the cost of care is substantial, often more than $100,000 a year, and most seniors simply cannot afford to pay for their care out of pocket for more than a month or two.

- Is there a difference between being admitted to a nursing home and staying at home with a registered caregiver?
- Who determines if you are able to receive benefits? Your physician? The insurance company?
- Is the coverage the same if you stay at home as opposed to being admitted to a nursing home?

An alternative to a standard type of insurance policy is to deposit a single sum or make deposits over ten years into a special type of annuity that will pay out a percentage of the total value for your care either at home or a nursing home. If the entire fund is not used during your lifetime, the balance of the benefits will go to your heirs.

Standalone home health-care policies are much less expensive than nursing home/home health-care policies. They are designed to pay for care at home, not in a nursing home, and have two advantages:

1. The patient can be kept in his/her own comfortable surroundings.
2. The cost of the protection is far less.

Policies can be designed to pay benefits for one year up to a lifetime. Benefits can be set to start immediately or put off for up to 365 days. The shorter the benefit period and the longer the elimination period, the lower your cost will be.

For example, a sixty-year-old, healthy, nonsmoking male, using A F & L Insurance Company and starting coverage from day one with benefits extending a lifetime, would pay $830 per month for a home health-care policy. Using Physicians Mutual Insurance with benefits starting after 365 days and extending only one year, the cost would be $157 for the year. Of course there are many alternatives between these extremes.*

Many different kinds of insurance scams target seniors. The National Association of Insurance Commissioners, *http://www.naic.org/*, provides information and links to help you avoid being scammed.

---

*This information was supplied by Gil Nickelson, CLU, ChFC, SFS and is based on 2004 quotes which could increase in subsequent years.

Choosing a Nursing Home

For help in choosing a nursing home, negotiating fees, resolving billing questions, or finding assisted living quarters, look at Senior CareGuiders: *http://www.careguiders.com/*.

The Medicare Web site, *http://www.medicare.gov/*, is a good resource to help you find nursing homes convenient to the location you are looking for.

The website *http://myhealthcareadvisor.com/* can help you choose a hospital and make health-care decisions but there is a small charge (at publication time it was $12 for a six-month subscription) to subscribe and get answers to your questions. Powered by Subimo, hospitals are ranked from 1 to 100 based on a number of factors including use of technology and cost. The information provided on the site says, "The Healthcare Advisor is a powerful personal health management tool, integrating cost and quality information to help you make better health care decisions. Whether you're looking for information on a common medical condition or procedure or where to go for treatment, the Healthcare Advisor empowers you to make the right choice by presenting what you need to know clearly and simply."

For additional resources, contact one of these organizations:

AARP: *http://www.aarp.org/ppi*

Home Renovations for the Elderly: *http://www.homemods.org/*

Consumer Consortium on Assisted Living, *http://www.ccal.org/*

National Association for Homecare and Hospice: *http://www.nahc.org/*

National Center for Assisted Living: *http://www.ncal.org/*

Assisted Living Federation of America: *http://www.alfa.org/*

Total Living Choices: *http://www.tlchoices.com/*

National Alliance for Care Giving: *http://www.caregiving.org/*

National Family Caregivers Associations: *http://www.nfcacares.org/*

Caring from a Distance: *http://www.cfad.org/*

Center for Medicaid & Medicare Services: *http://www.medicare.gov/*

Alzheimer's Association: *http://www.alz.org/*

Oncolink (cancer help): *http://www.oncolink.upenn.edu/*

Aging Network Services: *http://www.agingnets.com/*

Eldercare Locator: *http://www.eldercare.gov/Eldercare/Public/Home.asp*

SeniorBridge Family: *http://www.seniorbridgefamily.com/*

National Association of Professional Geriatric Care Managers: *http://www.caremanager.org/*, 520-881-8008

National Academy of Elder Law Attorneys: *http://www.naela.org/*, 520-881-4005

Help from an Ombudsman

Under the federal Older Americans Act, every state must have an advocate for residents of long-term and related facilities. Ombudsmen can assist in finding facilities, as they are generally very familiar with homes in their area. They can also help file complaints about care, as long as the resident agrees to disclose the information. To locate your state's ombudsman, go to National Association of State Long-Term Care Ombudsman Programs, *www.ltcombudsman.org*.

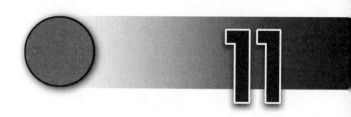

Live Better and Longer

Chapter Overview

- Research to Live Longer
- Dietary Guidelines
- Healthy Foods to Eat
- General Advice
- Helpful Medical Web Sites

All seniors want to live better, of course, but most of us want to live longer only if our quality of life is a good one. This chapter explores some of the ways that should help you have a better quality of life as you age and directs you to resources that will assist you to do so.

Research to Live Longer

Research has shown that keeping active (physically and mentally), eating healthy, and taking care of your body by not smoking, not drinking excessively, and not eating too much are all contributing factors to quality of life. Diets low in sodium and fats and high in fruits and vegetables, particularly those high in fiber and antioxidants, help many people live longer; in some cases, limiting caffeine intake does likewise. We have read that people who regularly drink red wine or regularly eat certain kinds of fish live longer, healthier lives.

Deciding what to eat and what not to eat is difficult with so many conflicting studies. Below you will find some recent information along these lines that I hope is not too confusing. I, for one, have been eating this way for some time now: the right fish with a dish of tomatoes, and washing it down with a glass of red wine.

A number of studies and research recently conducted suggest that eating certain kinds of fish is inversely related to the risks of stroke and heart attacks. Even if you eat fish as little as two or three times a month you may get some protection. Fish like tuna reduces the risk of coronary heart disease because of its content of omega-3 fatty acids. On the other hand, fish like swordfish, orange roughy, red snapper, shark, and mackerel often have high mercury levels that can cause other medical problems.

Foods that contain lycopene, like tomatoes, help to reduce the risk of developing arteriosclerosis and coronary heart disease, according to some research, and also help with LDL cholesterol. Still other research has shown that drinking red wine in moderation decreases the production of a protein that causes blood vessels to reduce the flow of oxygen to the heart.

Dietary Guidelines

Diets that include at least ten servings of fruits and vegetables per day might help prevent age-related damage to cells. Fruits and veggies, the more colorful the better, contain protective substances that might help ward off diseases such as cancer and heart disease. Most longevity experts recommend cutting down on fatty, salty foods. Go for lean meats, poultry, and fish, as well as a wide variety of fresh fruits, veggies, and whole-grain foods.

The U.S. advisory panel revamping the government's dietary guidelines now recommends that Americans eat at least three cups of dark green vegetables, like broccoli or spinach; two cups of orange vegetables, like carrots and squash; three cups of legumes, like lentils and chickpeas; six cups of starchy vegetables like potatoes, corn, and green beans; and seven cups of other vegetables, like tomatoes, onions, and lettuce per week.

As to losing weight the panel wrote, "The healthiest way to reduce calorie intake is to reduce one's intake of added sugars, solid fat and alcohol—they all provide calories, but they do not provide essential nutrients."

Living longer and having a better quality of life is a subject addressed by countless experts and nonexperts alike. President Bill Clinton commented in his book *My Life* about a biology lesson at Georgetown University that stuck with him, and was later confirmed in a 2000 study. His professor claimed life was shortened by the body's inability to absorb and dispose of food. He recommended greatly lowering the quantity of food eaten by older people.

The American Dietetic Association's Web site, *http://www.eatright.org/Public/*, has a link for finding a nutrition professional. Also, to locate a registered dietitian in your area, ask your physician or call the consumer nutrition hotline (800-366-1655) of the National Center for Nutrition and Dietetics.

Healthy Foods to Eat

Curry

Consider increasing the amount of curry in your diet. In any case it wouldn't hurt. India has the world's lowest incidence of Alzheimer's disease and is by far the largest consumer per capita of curry. The University of Texas M. D. Anderson Cancer Center in Houston found that curcumin, one of the main biologically active chemicals in turmeric, not only inhibits the growth of melanoma cells in vitro but also induces the cells to "commit suicide." So curry may also help lower your risk of some cancers as well.

Here is my Cousin Mike's recipe for curry with cauliflower:

    3 tablespoons of oil (canola or vegetable)

    1 teaspoon of mustard seeds

    2 cloves of chopped garlic

    1 teaspoon of ground cumin

    tops (or florets) from a pound of cauliflower

    $1/2$ teaspoon of powdered ginger

    1 tablespoon of curry powder

    $1/2$ teaspoon salt

    $1/4$ teaspoon black pepper

    1 green chili, seeded and minced

    $1/4$ teaspoon ground turmeric

    $1/4$ teaspoon red chili powder

    $1/4$ cup of water

    fresh chopped coriander (to taste)

Heat oil in a sauce pan. When oil is hot, add mustard seeds and sauté for about a minute, then add the garlic and cumin and sauté for an additional minute. Put in the cauliflower, stirring for 4 minutes. Turn heat down and stir in powdered ginger, curry powder, salt, pepper, the minced green chili, turmeric, and red chili powder. Stir for a minute, add water, and allow to simmer on low heat for 20 minutes. Sprinkle with fresh chopped coriander and serve with white rice. A few raisins and banana go well with curry, as does mango chutney.

Blueberries

Blueberries, which are high in antioxidants, have been recommended as a healthy addition to the diet. My neighbor Dave Thomas is a fantastic baker and has let me include his recipe for blueberry pie as a great way to get your blueberry fix. His recipe is low in fat and low in calories for such a great-tasting pie:

Crust

- $2^{1}/_{2}$ cups of flour
- $^{1}/_{2}$ teaspoon of salt
- $^{1}/_{2}$ cup of butter (prefer unsalted for health reasons)
- $^{1}/_{3}$ cup Crisco
- 1 tablespoon of granulated sugar
- 6 teaspoons of cold water
- Additional flour to sprinkle on

Combine flour and salt and mix in a food processor. Add butter and Crisco and mix again until well mixed. Add sugar and mix for a couple of seconds. Sprinkle with 3 tablespoons of cold water. Mix again for short period of time (5 seconds or so) and add remainder of water 1 tablespoon at a time until dough clumps. Place the dough on a lightly floured counter and shape it into 2 flat cakes. Wrap in foil and place in refrigerator for 30 minutes.

Filling

    3 cups of flour
    1 tablespoon of cornstarch
    pinch of salt
    1 cup of granulated sugar
    1 tablespoon of lemon juice
    $1/2$ teaspoon cinnamon (ground)
    5 cups blueberries (medium sized) or 5 1/2 cups small

Pre-heat oven at 350 degrees. In a large bowl combine the flour, cornstarch, salt, sugar, lemon juice, and cinnamon. Stir gently. Add blueberries and toss gently. On a lightly floured board roll one piece of dough to 10 inches in diameter. Lift the dough onto the rolling pin and ease it into a 9-inch pie pan, letting the excess dough hang over the side. Spoon the fruit mixture into the dough. Cut up the butter and dot the fruit mixture with it. Roll the other piece of dough to 9 inches in diameter. Lift it onto the fruit mixture. Crimp the top and bottom edges together.

    Set the pie on a rimmed baking sheet and bake for 1 hour or until the juices are bubbling at the edges and the crust is golden. Cool for at least 30 minutes and serve with a thick wedge of ice cream on top. (Ice milk or no-sugar-added ice cream would be better for you.)

    One of my favorite ways to eat blueberries is to mix them with sour cream (nonfat yogurt can be substituted) and brown sugar (lite brown sugar or brown sugar substitute can be used), chill and serve.

General Advice

While doing research on how seniors can help avoid heart attacks I came across several studies that spoke about health risk factors. They all seem to agree with cardiologists who recommend that you should:

- Lower your cholesterol with proper diet, exercise, and medication if necessary
- Avoid abnormal obesity with proper diet and exercise
- Avoid depression
- Avoid excess stress
- Quit smoking
- Bring your blood pressure down
- Avoid diabetes; if you have it, make sure to treat it under doctor's orders

If you can change your lifestyle to avoid these risk factors, you should certainly be less likely to have a heart attack. In many cases the advice of a physician or specialist will be helpful or necessary to assist you.

If you are interested in finding out the chances of developing heart disease, stroke, diabetes, osteoporosis, and twelve varieties of cancer check out Harvard University's Schools of Public Health Web site, *http://www.yourdiseaserisk.harvard.edu/*. You must fill out a questionnaire, and the site will give you information as well as ways you might reduce your risk.

The Department of Health and Human Services has a Web tool that allows you to track family health patterns that might signal a higher risk for cancer or some other diseases: *http://www.hhs.gov/familyhistory/*.

The National Society of Genetic Counselors has a data base to help you find a genetic counselor in your area: *http://www.nsgc.org/resourcelink.asp*.

The American Academy of Family Physicians provides a list of recommended tests that everyone over 50 should regularly undergo: *http://familydoctor.org/x4959.xml*.

If, after all this good advice, you need to go into the hospital, go to Subimo.com for a ranking of hospitals on a 0–100 scale, go to *MyUHC.com* for recommending patients with significant problems to specific hospitals.

Go to *Healthgrades.com* for ratings of hospitals. Once you have selected a hospital based on this rating system you much pay $9.95 for a more detailed report.

Helpful Medical Web Sites

According to *Business Week*'s Carol Marie Cropper at *http://www.businessweek.com/execlife*, the best medical Web sites are as follows:

- *http://www.nlm.nih.gov/*—National Library of Medicine, part of the government's National Institutes of Health. Also check out health sites such as Medline Plus, a patient-friendly location for looking up drugs and medical conditions which also gives the latest health news and a link for information on clinical trials in your area.
- *http://www.nimh.nih.gov/*—National Institute of Mental Health, which is part of the National Institutes of Health and provides a comprehensive and authoritative source of information on mental disorders and treatments.
- *http://www.health.gov/*—U.S. Health & Human Services Department offers well-organized information on everything from breast-feeding to menopause as well as new items on women's health.
- *http://www.mayoclinic.com/*—Mayo Foundation for Medical Education & Research, an affiliate of the Mayo Clinic of Rochester, Minnesota. This comprehensive site guides patients who are weighing treatment options. Tools let you calculate everything from body mass index to pregnancy due date (for your pending grandchildren).
- *http://www.nationalhealthcouncil.org/*—From a nonprofit made up of voluntary health agencies, professional associations, and medical nonprofits and businesses, this site is a one-stop directory of links to groups like the American Cancer Society, the American Heart

Association, and the National Hospice & Palliative Care Organization.
- *http://www.yourdiseaserisk.harvard.edu/*—from the Harvard Center for Cancer Prevention, at the Harvard School of Public Health. Readers can fill out online questionnaires for quick assessments of their risk for diabetes, heart disease, osteoporosis, stroke, and various cancers. The site ranks your risk factors.
- *http://www.drugdigest.org/DD/Home*—Express Scripts, a major pharmacy benefits manager. Allows users to check for potential interactions between the drugs they use as well as with food and alcohol. Also lets users compare side effects of different drugs. Site tells whether a generic is available, provides a picture of the pill, and cites uses for the medication.
- *http://www.questdiagnostics.com/*—Quest Diagnostics is a leading diagnostics testing company. Its health library offers information on medical tests, medication, support groups, and general health topics.
- *http://www.oncolink.com/*—Abramson Cancer Center of the University of Pennsylvania. Its library provides physician summaries of the journal articles that have influenced the standard of care for various types of cancer, as well as free access to the table of contents and abstracts from many cancer-related journals.

Cancer Tests and Danger Signs

Tests are often recommended for various kinds of cancers, including breast, colorectal, lung, oral, prostate, and others. Additional sites offer general guidelines about which tests to take and what to talk about with your physician to assist you in identifying cancer at an early stage. Two helpful Web sites are from the American Cancer Society, *http://www.cancer.org/*, and U.S. Preventative Services Task Force, *www.ahrq.gov*.

Specific tests for cancer include mammography, digital mammography, tomosynthesis breast imaging MRIs, PET scans (positron emission tomography), CT scans (X-ray computer tomography), 3D and Doppler ultrasounds. fecal occult blood tests, flexible sigmoidoscopy, double contrast barium enema and colonoscopy, spiral CT scans, and PSA tests.

Your physician should give you more information on these tests and how often they should be administered depending on your symptoms (if any), physical condition, age, and risk factors.

According to the American Cancer Society here are some of the common signs associated with different types of cancer:

Breast Cancer
- A lump or swelling in the breast
- Nipple pain or the nipple turning inward
- Redness, scaliness of the nipple or breast skin
- Discharge from the nipple other than breast milk

Lung Cancer
- A cough that does not go away
- Chest pain
- Hoarseness
- Bloody or rust-colored spit or phlegm

Ovarian Cancer
- Bloating or fullness in the abdomen
- Unusual abdominal or lower back pain
- Unusual lack of energy
- Constipation or diarrhea

Prostate Cancer
- Blood in the urine
- Impotence
- Pain in the hips, spine, ribs
- Loss of bladder or bowel control

Colorectal Cancer
- Change in bowel habits, such as diarrhea or constipation, that lasts for more than a few days

- Rectal bleeding or blood in the stool
- Cramping or steady pain in the abdominal area
- Weakness or fatigue

Oral Cancer
- Sore or pain in the mouth that does not go away
- Difficulty chewing or swallowing
- Lump or mass in the neck
- Persistent white or red patch on the gums, tongue, tonsils or lining of the mouth

Pancreatic Cancer
- Jaundice
- Diabetes mellitus (high blood sugar)
- Pain in the abdomen or back
- Digestive problems

Skin Cancers
- Although only about one thousand to two thousand people a year die from basal and squamous cell carcinomas, these kinds of skin cancers are becoming more common. They can also be disfiguring even if they don't spread. About 90 percent of these cancers typically appear on the head and neck. However, more and more cases are appearing on other parts of the body, probably reflecting the effects of excessive exposure to the sun. Seniors who have spent a great deal of time outdoors are most at risk and are advised to visit a dermatologist regularly to have their skin checked thoroughly.

Other Health Issues

For other information about health issues, the following Web sites are also helpful:

- To download information on psychosocial as well as financial issues related to the elderly: *http://www.drugs.com/*
- Information on health: *http://www.health.nih.gov/*
- Senior health issues: *http://nihseniorhealth.gov/*

- Symptoms: *http://www.emedicinehealth.com/*
- A to Z index of health topics: *http://www.cdc.gov/*
- Lists of patient assistance programs: *http://www.needymeds.com/*
- Physicians' Desk Reference: *http://www.pdrhealth.com/*
- PhRMA Clinical Study Results: *http://www.clinicalstudyresults.org/*
- FDA MedWatch: *http://www.fda.gov/medwatch/*
- National Institutes of Health's MedlinePlus: *http://www.medlineplus.gov/*
- Public Citizen's Worst Pills: *http://www.worstpills.org/*
- Food & Drug Administration's Center for Drug Evaluation: *http://www.fda.gov/cder/*
- National Library of Medicine: *http://www.ncbi.nlm.nih.gov/entrez/query.fcgi*
- WebMD: *http://www.webmd.com/*
- Express Scripts library—info on more than fifteen hundred drugs: *http://www.drugdigest.org/*

A number of sites also assist those suffering from various diseases. As an example there is an excellent site that provides information on managing chemotherapy. Check out *http://www.procrit.com/oncology/diagnosed/registration.jsp*, which also includes tips on what not to eat, etc.

Another worthwhile reference is *The Strength for Living* newsletter published by Ortho Biotech Products, L.P.

12

Memory Loss

Chapter Overview

- Memory Loss Defined
- What Should Concern You
- Ten Ways to Maintain Your Brain
- Ten Warning Signs of Alzheimer's Disease
- Simple Memory Lapses Are Not Alzheimer's

Of all things that seem to bother seniors, memory loss is at the top of the list.

From just an occasional "senior moment" to worrying whether you are in the beginning stages of Alzheimer's, most of us give memory loss a great deal of thought. When I began writing this book, almost without exception, my friends asked me to include this chapter.

Memory Loss Defined

According to the *Medical Encyclopedia* memory loss (amnesia) is defined as unusual forgetfulness that can be caused by brain damage due to disease or injury, or it can be caused by severe emotional trauma.

The cause determines whether amnesia comes on slowly or suddenly, and whether it is temporary or permanent. Normal aging may result in trouble learning new material or requiring longer time to recall learned material. However, it does not lead to dramatic memory loss unless diseases are involved.

As we get older, we have more and more "senior moments." I know I do. Some of our loss of memory is real, and some is imagined. Once you get to thinking about the things you can't remember, it seems this happens more often than when you were younger.

Of course you can do lots of things to help you remember. I suggest that you start making lists. I find that writing things down helps me to remember them, and if I can remember where I put my list, this helps too.

Keeping a calendar day by day is great for not missing appointments, birthdays, anniversaries, and so on. I also find that if I put my "stuff" in exactly the same place all the time, I can always find it. This is particularly true with respect to glasses, keys, wallet, and the TV remote. "A place for everything and everything in its place" should be your motto.

One of the most frustrating senior moments is not being able to remember names—the restaurant you want to go to for dinner, your cousin's little boy, the name of the city your friend Joe lives in. A little "crib" of names and places helps a lot. In almost all cases you will think of what you have been trying to remember in time. When you do, write it down in your "crib" as you will probably need to recall this name again in a day or week or two.

Memory loss in most cases is not serious. It's just aggravating. Of course many of us worry that having difficulty remembering something might be the beginning of Alzheimer's. A very small percentage of seniors over 65 have Alzheimer's, but this percentage increases to almost 30 percent once you reach 85, according to the Medical College of Wisconsin. Other research shows this percentage even higher.

What Should Concern You

I searched a number of authoritative Web sites and publications for a list of things you should be concerned about if you feel your memory is slipping. They all listed the same kinds of things:

1. Difficulty learning new things
2. Difficulty making change and handling money in general
3. Forgetting things more often than you did last month or last year
4. Forgetting how to do things you have been doing for years
5. Repeating yourself over and over again
6. Inability to remember what happens each day

If you are faced with any of these difficulties regularly, you should see your physician.

On the other hand, some forgetfulness is quite normal. We all forget things occasionally at any age, and it is normal to forget more often as you get older. What must be determined by your physician is the difference between normal memory loss and that which occurs when you have a more serious condition, like age-associated memory loss impairment, dementia, or Alzheimer's.

Ten Ways to Maintain Your Brain™

The following list came from the Alzheimer's Association Web site, *http://www.alz.org/maintainyourbrain/overview.asp*:

1. Head first! Good health starts with your brain. It's one of the most vital body organs, and it needs care and maintenance.
2. Take brain health to heart. What's good for the heart is good for the brain. Do something every day to prevent heart disease, high blood pressure, diabetes, and stroke—all of which can increase your risk of Alzheimer's.
3. Your numbers count. Keep your body weight, blood pressure, cholesterol, and blood sugar levels within recommended ranges.
4. Feed your brain. Eat less fat and more antioxidant-rich foods.
5. Work your body. Physical exercise keeps the blood flowing and may encourage new brain cells. Do what you can—like walking thirty minutes a day—to keep both body and mind active.
6. Jog your mind. Keeping your brain active and engaged increases its vitality and builds reserves of brain cells and connections. Read, write, play games, learn new things, do crossword puzzles.
7. Connect with others. Leisure activities that combine physical, mental, and social elements may be most likely to prevent dementia. Be social, converse, volunteer, join a club, or take a class.
8. Heads up! Protect your brain. Take precautions against head injuries. Use your car seat belts, unclutter your house to avoid falls, and wear a helmet when cycling.
9. Use your head. Avoid unhealthy habits. Don't smoke, drink excessive alcohol, or use street drugs.
10. Think ahead—start today! You can do something today to protect your tomorrow.

Ten Warning Signs of Alzheimer's Disease

To help family members and health-care professionals recognize the warning signs of Alzheimer's disease, the Alzheimer's Association has developed a checklist of common symptoms.

1. **Memory loss.** One of the most common early signs of dementia is forgetting recently learned information. While it's normal to forget appointments, names, or telephone numbers, those with dementia will forget such things more often and not remember them later.
2. **Difficulty performing familiar tasks.** People with dementia often find it hard to complete everyday tasks that are so familiar we usually do not think about how to do them. A person with Alzheimer's may not know the steps for preparing a meal, using a household appliance or participating in a lifelong hobby.
3. **Problems with language.** Everyone has trouble finding the right word sometimes, but a person with Alzheimer's often forgets simple words or substitutes unusual words, making his or her speech or writing hard to understand. If a person with Alzheimer's is unable to find his or her toothbrush, for example, the individual may ask for "that thing for my mouth."
4. **Disorientation to time and place.** It's normal to forget the day of the week or where you're going. But people with Alzheimer's disease can become lost on their own street. They may forget where they are and how they got there, and may not know how to get back home.
5. **Poor or decreased judgment.** No one has perfect judgment all of the time. Those with Alzheimer's may dress without regard to the weather, wearing several shirts on a warm day or very little clothing in cold weather. Those with dementia often show poor judgment about money, giving away large sums to telemarketers or paying for home repairs or products they don't need.

6. **Problems with abstract thinking.** Balancing a checkbook is a task that can be challenging for some. But a person with Alzheimer's may forget what the numbers represent and what needs to be done with them.
7. **Misplacing things.** Anyone can temporarily misplace a wallet or key. A person with Alzheimer's disease may put things in unusual places, like an iron in the freezer or a wristwatch in the sugar bowl.
8. **Changes in mood or behavior.** Everyone can become sad or moody from time to time. Someone with Alzheimer's disease can show rapid mood swings—from calm to tears to anger—for no apparent reason.
9. **Changes in personality.** Personalities ordinarily change somewhat with age. But a person with Alzheimer's can change dramatically, becoming extremely confused, suspicious, fearful or dependent on a family member.
10. **Loss of initiative.** It's normal to tire of housework, business activities or social obligations at times. The person with Alzheimer's disease may become very passive, sitting in front of the television for hours, sleeping more than usual or not wanting to do usual activities.

If you recognize any warning signs in yourself or a loved one, the Alzheimer's Association recommends consulting a physician. Early diagnosis of Alzheimer's disease or other disorders causing dementia is an important step to getting appropriate treatment, care and support services.

Simple Memory Lapses Are Not Alzheimer's

Symptoms of Alzheimer's disease are much more severe than such simple memory lapses. Alzheimer symptoms are progressive, affecting communication, learning, thinking, and reasoning. Eventually they impact on a person's work and social life.

What's the difference?

Someone with Alzheimer's symptoms	Someone with normal age-related memory changes
Forgets entire experiences	Forgets part of an experience
Rarely remembers later	Often remembers later
Is gradually unable to follow written/spoken directions	Is usually able to follow written/spoken directions
Is gradually unable to use notes as reminders	Is usually able to use notes as reminders
Is gradually unable to care for self	Is usually able to care for self

For more information about Alzheimer's research, treatment and care, contact the Alzheimer's Association. Additional information on memory loss can be found by visiting the American Geriatrics Society at *http://www.americangeriatrics.org/*, which answers commonly asked questions by concerned seniors, such as:

- I can't remember things like I used to. Should I be concerned?
- What causes memory problems?
- Should I see a doctor if I have trouble with my memory?
- What will the doctor do?
- What if I complete a screening test and the results are normal or borderline?
- What if the test is abnormal?
- What if I have probable Alzheimer's disease?

Current research on Alzheimer's, memory loss, and aging, including a list of symptoms and treatment, can be found on the Medical College of Wisconsin's Web site, ***http://healthlink.mcw.edu/article/980547889.html***.

The Alzheimer's disease Education and Referral Center can be contacted at 800-438-4380, or by e-mail at: *adear@alzheimers.org*.

The Alzheimer's Association can be reached at 800-272-3900, or *http://www.alz.org/*.

13

Get a Pet

Chapter Overview

- Choosing a Dog
  The Breed for You
  Selecting a Breeder
  How Much Does a Puppy Cost?
  Dog Ownership Equals Responsibility
  Caring for Your Dog
  Your Dog and Your Neighbors
  Obedience Training for Everyone
- Choosing a Cat
  Pedigree or Non-Pedigree?
  Long or Short Hair?
  Male or Female?
  One Cat or More?
  Where to Get Your Cat
  What to Look For
- Adopt a Pet
- Losing Your Pet

After you retire you have more time to take care of a dog or cat. Some say that your dog or cat actually takes care of you, but remember that providing care for furry friends can be expensive. If you are not prepared to spend the money for veterinary care if your little guy or gal needs attention, you should instead spend the time with a friend's or relative's dog or cat.

Choosing a Dog

Thinking about buying a dog? Critter Haven (*http://www.critterhaven.org/infopak.htm*) provides excellent information on getting a dog. This information is provided free, sponsored by Critter Haven, Inc., to help all who want a companion animal in their life, to do their homework, to research the breed they are looking for, and by all means to educate the public on the reasons they should *not* buy a puppy from a pet store.

Owning a dog can bring years of happiness as the special bond between humans and canines exceeds even the greatest of expectations. However, to ensure the best relationship with your dog, you must be prepared for some important responsibilities. Keep the following questions in mind as we go along.

- Have you found the right breed to fit into your lifestyle and home?
- Will you have enough time to spend training, grooming, and exercising a dog?
- Are you willing to spend the resources to ensure the best future for a dog?

The Breed for You

Is there a breed you have had your eye on, or are you confused about how to select a dog? In either case, you should do some homework to make sure that you select the right dog for you and your family. The bonus of selecting a purebred dog is their predictability in size, coat, care requirements, and temperament. Knowing what your cute puppy will look like and the kind of care he or she will need as an adult is a key in selecting the breed for you.

Too frequently, common sense goes out the window when it comes to buying a puppy. This seems to be even truer when the purchase is by a family with children. Buying a dog is like buying anything else; the more you know before you buy, the better off you will be. This advice applies to all aspects of buying your dog, from selecting the breed to deciding where to obtain the puppy. We strongly recommend that you spend enough time investigating before buying. Remember, dogs are for life.

The American Kennel Club's *Complete Dog Book* can help you begin your research with its pictures and descriptions of each breed recognized by the AKC. Your initial research will help you narrow the field when it comes to selecting the breed for you and your lifestyle. Remember to consider your dog's lifestyle, too. For extended research, consult the resources at your local library.

While investigating, always be honest with yourself. The Bearded Collie you fell in love with because of his lush coat is indeed beautiful, but are you going to be able to brush this coat every day, as it requires? Maybe a short-coated dog better suits your lifestyle. Think about the size of your house or your apartment. Will that golden retriever be happy in your studio apartment? The golden retriever is a larger sporting dog that requires a lot of exercise. Do you have a fenced yard so he can go out safely? If not, can you afford to install a fence? These are crucial questions regarding the safety of your dog and being a responsible neighbor.

Always remember, it is okay to change your mind about which breed you want or if you want the responsibility of owning a dog at all. Owning a dog is a big responsibility! Talk to breeders. Ask them lots of questions; we all know there are no stupid questions. A responsible breeder will eagerly answer your questions and share his or her experience and knowledge with you. Where can you find breeders and see dogs? At dog shows. Also contact AKC clubs in your area for their recommendations.

Selecting a Breeder

Buy your puppy from a responsible and well-respected breeder. This point cannot be stressed enough. Responsible breeders are concerned with the betterment of the breed. For example, they work on breeding healthier dogs with the appropriate temperament for their breed. Your AKC breeder referral contact will direct you to a breeder who is concerned with the future of the puppy. Once you select a breeder, screen the breeder. Ask to see at least one of the parents (the dam or the sire) of your puppy. See how the dogs in your breeder's home interact with your breeder. Are they friendly and outgoing, or do they shy away? The responsible breeder will be screening you, too, looking for the best home for each puppy.

How Much Does a Puppy Cost?

Now is not the time to hunt for a bargain. Your new puppy will be a member of your family for his lifetime, so you'll want to make a wise investment.

The purchase price of your puppy is not the only cost you have to consider. Be aware that the puppy you bring home will need proper care in these areas: food and health care (a dog needs annual shots, for example). Your puppy will also need little things like a collar with identification, a bowl, and a leash. Evaluate your budget; ask yourself if you really can afford a dog.

Dog Ownership Equals Responsibility

Take the time to ask yourself these questions and to make an educated decision. You and your dog will be happier for it. There is no doubt that a puppy is a cuddly bundle of joy, but it is also a huge responsibility.

Caring for Your Dog

All dogs must be cared for daily. This means proper diet, exercise, grooming, and veterinary attention. There are many

Get a Pet

excellent guides on all facets of dog care. AKC's own books, *The Complete Dog Book* and *Dog Care and Training*, contain information on proper dog care. We recommend you have these or some other authoritative reference source available. Do not attempt to be your own veterinarian! All dogs should be regularly examined by a veterinarian and inoculated against the major infectious canine diseases.

Your Dog and Your Neighbors
All dog owners must be aware of their responsibilities to their neighbors, both those who live in the area immediately around their residence and their neighbors in the broader sense of the community as a whole. Dogs, for all the pleasure they are, can be a nuisance to your neighbors if not trained. Remember, excessive barking can be annoying. Always keep your dog on a leash or inside a fenced yard when exercising. Remember to pick up after your dog. Forestall problems for yourself and your dog and all dog lovers by being a good neighbor.

Obedience Training for Everyone
One way to make your dog a good neighbor is through obedience training. A poorly behaved dog is a problem for everyone. Nothing is more frustrating than attempting to corral a dog that will not "come" when you call. A well-trained dog is not only a pleasure to own, he is a goodwill ambassador for the entire canine community. A well-behaved dog is the result of the dog's owner being willing to work with the dog regularly in a systematic manner. Obedience classes are available in most communities. Time spent training your dog is time well spent.

Choosing a Cat
The Whiskas Web site (*www.whiskas.com*) provides good information on getting a cat and includes the following:

After you've made up your mind to get a cat, should you get a purebred cat or a non-purebred cat? Should it be longhaired or shorthaired, male or female? You may even be wondering if you should get two or more cats, either for your own enjoyment or so your cat will never be alone. Here are a few tips to help you choose a cat:

Pedigree or Non-Pedigree?
There are between forty and eighty different cat breeds and about five hundred varieties within these breeds. Characteristics vary enormously among breeds. Just look at the ever-popular Siamese, Burmese, and Persian, the Manx who has no tail, or the hairless Canadian Sphinx. Apart from the differences in their appearance, each breed has a distinct temperament and personality. The Siamese, for example, is well known as an extrovert, whereas the longhaired Persians are generally more sedate.

Many books are available describing the characteristics of different breeds. On your fact-finding mission, you can check out the peculiarities of every breed. You'll also have a chance to meet all these different kinds of cats if you go to a cat show. There you can see what breed appeals to you most. Chances are, you'll see a lot of amazing and adorable cats you'll want to take home right on the spot!

Most cat owners don't choose a purebred. For most of us, non-purebred cats have all the attributes we're looking for, and come in a wide variety of different colors and coat types.

Long or Short Hair?
Longhaired cats can be very attractive. And just like people who have long hair, they need a lot of grooming attention. To keep their coat tangle-free and in good condition, they need regular grooming. So, part of the pleasure of owning a longhaired cat involves brushing her every day. Most cats love to be brushed and will purr while you brush them.

If you think you may not have the time every day to brush your cat, think twice about getting a longhaired cat. If you get a cat with a matted coat, you may need to take her to the vet to be clipped, because she may not feel particularly happy about having her coat untangled. You vet may sedate her so she won't be so uncomfortable.

Male or Female?

Male cats are generally larger than females. Uncastrated tomcats tend to go off wandering around the neighborhood and can get into fights with other cats. They may also mark their territory by "spraying" with their urine or by leaving their feces unburied. This may be normal behavior for them, but rather unpleasant for you as their owner!

Unneutered female cats will come into season regularly and may become pregnant. While they're in heat, they can be very loud, and the neighborhood tomcats will find them very attractive!

Unless you intend to breed your cat, it's best to have him or her neutered. Once they're neutered, there's no difference between male and female cats.

Here's something interesting: If you already have an adult cat and plan to get a new kitten, you may find that the new kitten is more readily accepted if he or she is of the opposite gender as your adult cat.

One Cat or More?

Many cat owners aren't sure whether it's best to have just one cat or more. This decision depends on the individual cat. Some cats prefer to live with other cats, while some much prefer to spend their time alone or with humans. If you already have an adult cat, you probably have a good idea of what she would prefer and how she would get along with another cat.

If you are away from home for much of the day, you may want to get two or more cats so they can keep each other company. Kittens who've been brought up together generally get along very well, even as adults.

The number of cats you can have also depends on the size of your home. Just like people, they need their own space and don't like to feel overcrowded. As a general rule, you should have at least one room for every cat you have, so they have space to retreat to if they want to be alone. You may also need a separate litter box for each cat, because some cats don't like to share their litter box with others.

Where to Get Your Cat

There are a number of sources for finding cats. Once you've decided to get a cat, start putting the word out among your friends and neighbors. One of them might have a cat or kittens for sale, or know of someone who does. Litters are often advertised in newspapers and shop windows. A big source for cats is animal shelters. They usually have many cats and kittens who desperately need homes.

Don't buy from a dealer who has bought kittens from several sources. They could have been weaned too early, and may have traveled long distances. The risk of disease and stress-induced illness is greater for these kittens. Since you can't be sure of the history and health status of cats in this situation, you should ask your vet for advice.

If you've decided to buy a purebred kitten, then the best source is from a recognized and reputable breeder. You can find these breeders through other cat owners, your veterinarian, ads in newspapers and cat magazines, or by visiting cat shows. Breeding clubs can put you in touch with reputable breeders in your area.

What to Look For

First, ask to see the kittens with their mother. This way, you can assess the mother's general health and temperament. Bear in mind that she may have lost a little condition through rearing her litter. Most important, you can make sure the kittens haven't been prematurely weaned or brought in from somewhere else.

It's best to wait until the kitten is at least eight weeks old before you take her from her mother. Breeders of purebred cats often prefer to keep the kittens until they are twelve weeks old. Try to see a number of different litters before you make your decision. Only buy from premises that appear hygienic (but don't expect conditions to be sterile!), and where the cats seem happy and in good condition.

Healthy kittens are usually curious, and will show interest in strangers. Choose a kitten that is lively and playful without being too aggressive. It's best not to choose a shy kitten that avoids contact with humans and other kittens. The socialization period in cats is believed to end at seven to nine weeks of age, so it's important that your kitten has been well socialized before she comes to live with you.

Choose a kitten that is active and looks healthy and clean. There should be no discharges from the eyes or nose. Make sure the ears are clean and the gums are a healthy pink color. Check for any signs of diarrhea under the tail or on the back legs. The coat should be clean with no areas of irritation. And don't think a kitten with a potbelly is cute; she may actually have worms. Also, an undersized kitten may have a medical problem. Check the vaccination and worming status of the kitten you choose, and make sure you are given any relevant certificates.

Adopt a Pet

If you don't already have a furry friend with which to share your life, take a trip to your local animal shelter and adopt a dog or cat that has already been trained. Animal shelters carefully screen the animals they put up for adoption for temperament as well as health. Adopted dogs and cats will have already received their necessary shots and inoculations.

In most cases it is better to stay away from pet stores. Those loveable dogs and cats in the window often have come from puppy farms and breeding dens and have problems you really don't want to get into. Of course you can also go to a breeder or check the classifieds.

Losing Your Pet

There are many sites to help you handle losing a furry member of your family, but the one I like best is Rainbow Bridge (*http://www.rainbowbridge.com/*). Go there; you'll feel better!

There are unfortunately situations when you can no longer care for your dog or cat. Sometimes you must move to a place that does not allow them. Sometimes it's just too much for you. Hopefully you have friends or relatives who can help. Some people put ads in the local newspaper. In any case this is a traumatic circumstance that you should plan for well in advance.

You can get information from your local Human Society. You can check with The Lander Pet Connection *http://www.webpan.com/petconnection/* that provides the following information on its Web site: "We love all animals, and have a deep and abiding respect for all kinds of life. We spay/neuter, pay for vet care, boarding/fostering for homeless strays, unclaimed "pound" dogs and cats. We maintain a list of unwanted pets and match them with people wanting to adopt. Since November 1998 not one healthy pet in our community has been euthanized due to our efforts! And a total of 2500 dogs and cats have been placed in new homes. We are non-profit 501 C-3organization and exist only on donations from caring animal lovers. Donations are tax deductible." You can also get help provided by Animals at Risk Care Sanctuary *http://www.aarcs.org/* located in Stanislaus County, California, a non-profit organization staffed entirely by volunteers. Click on "links" on this site for an excellent list of rescue and other U.S. organizations that can help.

If you are interested in providing funds out of your estate to care for your pet after you have passed on, *http://estateplanningforpets.org/legal-other.htm* will give you information, links, and reference material.

14

Funding Your Retirement

Chapter Overview

- Ways to Save Money
- Planning on When to Retire
- Check Your Pension
- Social Security
- Medicare
- Your IRA
- Wills
- Information on Taxes
- Trusts

Obviously as you get closer to retirement your investment strategies should change. By the same token, once you are retired, where you have your funds and how you generate income, and where you get money for everyday expenses should change substantially. Unfortunately we regularly hear how unscrupulous con men (and women) have separated seniors from their hard-earned savings. We have also heard that if it sounds too good to be true it usually is a bad investment, but far too few seniors take this advice to heart.

This section is not designed to tell you how to invest or where to invest, but rather gives you information that might help your thinking as well as links and contacts to provide strategies and help you with your decisions.

Ways to Save Money

In order to increase your savings and contributions to your retirement fund, if you can practice just a few of these ways to save money you can add substantially to your retirement fund. If you are already retired, following even some of these suggestions will increase the money you will have at the end of each week.

- Open a home-equity line of credit and use it to pay off any credit card debt. Home-equity interest rates are far less than those of credit cards.
- Save all your change and take it to the bank every other month, more often if it turns out to be a large amount.
- Buy regular gas as opposed to premium, as most cars do not require premium fuel.
- Set your thermostat a little lower in the winter and higher in the summer. Only a few degrees will save you 10 percent or more on your utility bills. You can also purchase a "setback" thermostat at a hardware store for $100 or less. This thermostat can automatically adjust the heat or cooling in your house, condo or apartment.
- Carefully check or have a friend check your phone bills

to make sure you are not being charged for services or equipment you don't use or should not have. Combine your communications bills to a single company to save money. Consider using a cell phone, if you have one, for all your LD calls, or check with your LD carrier to see if they have a plan for long-distance service that meets your needs and your budget.
- Purchase second-hand cars. The cost savings are substantial, and if you purchase from a reputable dealer or have the car thoroughly checked by a mechanic prior to purchase you should be able to save a great deal of money.
- Cut back on your entertainment, particularly on eating out at expensive restaurants. The money saved can be substantial over a period of time.
- If you smoke, stop. The increased cost of cigarettes makes stopping smoking a big savings.
- Purchase generic or store-brand substitutes for brand-name items. Over several years time the savings can be a great deal more than you would imagine.
- If you gamble more than small amounts, stop. You are gambling your future security.

Planning on When to Retire

To give you an idea of the longevity you can expect, this information from MetLife may surprise you. Today a person who reaches 65 has a life expectancy of 85, but the odds that he/she will live beyond 85 are 50 percent. The likelihood of one member of a 65-year-old couple living to age 97 is 25 percent. In view of these surprising statistics it is more important than ever to plan to not outlive your savings.

The rule of thumb is that you'll need 70 percent to 80 percent of your preretirement income. Of course this varies substantially depending on special needs and where you plan to retire.

Americans are choosing to retire later. A UBS AG survey shows that the percentage of Americans making the decision to wait until after the age of 62 has increased as follows:

1998 . . . . .36 percent

2002 . . . . .47 percent

2003 . . . . .57 percent

Americans are becoming concerned they will outlive their retirement savings and are making the decision to postpone retirement or continuing to work part-time or in temporary jobs after they retire. An online Savings Calculator (*http://moneycentral.msn.com/Investor/calcs/n_savapp/main.asp*) walks you through the steps needed to reach your retirement goals. It also helps you determine how much you can save. If you increase your employment income after retirement, it would be much easier to make ends meet.

Another possibility is purchasing an annuity. There are so many different kinds of annuities, it's best you check with your financial advisor or insurance agent to see which is the best one for you or even if this is the kind of investment you should consider. There are many good books on the subject should you wish to do your own research. Check out *The Annuity Advisor* by John L. Olsen and Michael E. Kitces, *Getting Started in Annuities* by Gordon K. Williamson, *The Complete Idiot's Guide to Buying Insurance and Annuities* by Brian Breuel, or *The Pocket Idiot's Guide to Annuities* by Ken Little.

According to ImmediateAnnuity.com $100,000 invested in a lifelong annuity will pay a 65-year-old man $639 a month. It will pay a 70-year-old woman $675 a month. And it will pay a 70-year-old man and woman (joint annuity and survivor) $585 a month. With these annuities, payments run out when you die, leaving nothing for heirs. Inflation also erodes the purchasing power of the payments.

Of course if you are interested in purchasing an annuity, make sure you are dealing with a well-established firm with a long track record, as you want to make sure they are still in business when you are 95.

In looking over your assets, as a general rule, the value of your home (check its approximate value, *http://www.domania.com/*) will often represent your largest single source. An earlier chapter addressed where seniors live and gave some information on cost of living. Here I'll address how to use your home as a source of income. Many retirees have paid off their homes and either owe nothing or have a very small mortgage. This is fine if you have no need of funds, but if you are short of money the equity in your home is a cost-effective way to generate cash.

If you sell your home and have lived in it for two of the past five years, federal tax law provides a one time $250,000 capital gains exclusion per person. That's $500,000 per married couple filing jointly for most situations. Thus your home is often a large percentage of your total net worth and can be used to generate a good deal of cash if you need it. In addition you may use this home sale capital gains exclusion about once every two years. For example you could downsize from a large home to a smaller one and then move to a still less expensive condo and avoid most or even all of any capital gains tax each time you moved.

If you are not interested in selling you can also re-mortgage. The key here is to go to a legitimate bank or mortgage company and get the best possible rate. If you do not need a major amount of cash you can get a low-interest line of credit using your home as collateral or get a second mortgage if you already have a first. Generally speaking it is a good idea to borrow against your home and pay off any credit card debt, which is almost always at a much higher interest rate.

Some retirees have found that a reverse mortgage is a cost-effective way to use the value in their home to their best advantage. AARP provides good information on reverse mortgages at *http://www.aarp.org/revmort/*. This link also gives you information on alternatives to a reverse mortgage and public assistance programs. Another source for information is the National Reverse Mortgage Lenders Association. This site provides all kinds of information on reverse mortgages as well as links to possible lenders: *http://www.reversemortgage.org/*.

The Home Equity Conversion Mortgage (HECM) is the only reverse mortgage insured by the federal government. According to AARP, "HECM loans generally provide the largest loan advances of any reverse mortgage. Often they provide a lot more cash than any other program. An HECM also gives you the most choices in how you can have the cash paid to you." In order to take advantage of an HECM reverse mortgage you must be 62 years of age or older.

> **Important Goals to Achieve**
>
> Investments should be tailored so you do not outlive your money.
>
> Investments must generate sufficient income to maintain the lifestyle you choose, or your lifestyle must be adjusted to the income your investments provide.
>
> Investments must be positioned and managed to provide for your family as well as your estate.

What is a reverse mortgage? It is a loan generally used by seniors to convert the equity in their homes into cash. There are several ways you can receive this money: all at once or in fixed monthly payments. Some seniors prefer to use a reverse mortgage as a line of credit. This is an excellent way to use the value of your home to make sure you have funds if and when you need them at a reasonable rate of interest. Check out *http://www.reverse.org/* for more information.

Most financial advisors will diversify your investments with a strategy that works in a down market as well as an up market. This often means that your returns will not be as great in order to provide more safety.

Q: What percentage of my investments should be in stocks vs. bonds, and should this percentage change as I get older?

A: The old rule of thumb is to subtract your age from 100 to reach the correct percentage. Thus if you are 60 you should have 40 percent in stock and if you are 80 you should have reduced this amount to 20 percent. Some financial analysts suggest inflation-indexed bonds for added protection.

Unless you are a sophisticated investor, the safest place for your assets is in mutual funds. You can purchase both stock funds and bond funds and leave the decisions with regard to individual stocks and bonds to the managers of these funds. Now the question is which funds should you consider? Do you select funds that are invested in growth stocks, income-producing stocks, or some combination of the two? Do you select funds that are invested in tax-free bonds, domestic bonds, or international bonds? All of these decisions should be based on your age, your financial needs, the amount you have to invest, and your tax status. Many investment counselors advise retirees who wish to invest in the stock market to put these moneys in index funds that mirror the Dow Jones averages or the S&P 500 as these mutual funds charge less in management fees and often outperform managed funds when fees and dividend reinvestments are considered.

The U.S. Treasury sells two fixed-income securities that compensate for inflation.

1. The Treasury Inflation-Protected Security or TIPS
2. I-bond (savings bonds)

The income generated from these investments is comparatively low, but they both guarantee that your capital will not be lost to inflation.

Here are some resources to help you make investment decisions.

https://www.fidelity.com/
http://www.axaonline.com/
http://www.wachoviainvestment.com/

Many seniors about to retire and even those who have just begun their retirement years are concerned about outliving their financial resources. They are also in the process of budgeting for the years to come. Here is some information that should prove helpful in assessing how your assets will provide for you in the years to come.

Check Your Pension

To check up on your pension, or to check a pension from a former employer, go to *http://www.pbgc.gov/*.

If you are worried about the health of the pension plan of your employer and you are allowed to do so, consider taking a lump-sum payment when you retire and invest the money safely yourself. Some pension plans allow for this. Many do not.

At what age do you plan to retire? Many overestimate how long they will be working and saving for retirement. Check where you stand. Go to: *http://cgi.money.cnn.com/tools/retirementplanner/retirementplanner.jsp*, fill in your age, desired retirement age, current income, and expected income needed when you retire and the site will give you projected answers.

Retirement income calculators are available at *http://www3.troweprice.com/ric/RIC/* and *http://www.ing.com/us/tools_calcs/retire/*.

The Social Security calculator, *http://www.ssa.gov/planners/calculators.htm*, gives you a ballpark monthly benefits estimate for early, regular, or delayed retirement as well as estimated disability and survivor benefits.

Social Security

In addition to its benefits calculator, the Social Security Web site, *http://www.ssa.gov/*, gives all kinds of worthwhile information including:

- How to apply for Social Security benefits and disability benefits

FUNDING YOUR RETIREMENT 159

- Retirement planning information
- How to record marriages, divorces, and name changes, as well as deaths in the family
- Forms downloads
- Publications for ordering or viewing

Sign up for a free electronic newsletter on Social Security matters. Call Social Security at 1-800-772-1213 or visit their Web site, where you can apply for benefits. Get the address of your local Social Security office, and get forms to request important documents, such as a Social Security Statement, a replacement Social Security or Medicare card, or a letter to confirm your benefit amount.

For valuable booklets from Social Security, go to *http://www.ssa.gov/pubs/10035.html*, an electronic booklets Web site, and click on the links to get information on:

- Social Security and your retirement plans
- Your retirement benefits
- Family benefits
- What you need to know when you become eligible for retirement benefits

Below we have included some of the information from this site for those who do not have access to the Internet.

Social Security and Your Retirement Plan

Social Security is part of the retirement plan of almost every American worker. If you are among the 96 percent of workers who are covered under Social Security, you should know how the system works and what you should receive from Social Security when you retire. This booklet explains how you qualify for Social Security benefits, how your earnings and age can affect your benefits, what you should think about in deciding when to retire and why you should not count only on Social Security for your retirement income.

This booklet provides basic information on Social Security retirement benefits and is not intended to answer all questions.

For specific information about your situation, you should talk with a Social Security representative.

How Do You Qualify for Retirement Benefits?
When you work and pay Social Security taxes, you earn "credits" toward Social Security benefits. The number of credits you need to get retirement benefits depends on when you were born. If you were born in 1929 or later, you need 40 credits (10 years of work). If you stop working before you have enough credits to qualify for benefits, the credits will remain on your Social Security record. If you return to work later on, you can add more credits so that you qualify. No retirement benefits can be paid until you have the required number of credits.

How Much Will Your Retirement Benefit Be?
Your benefit payment is based on how much you earned during your working career. Higher lifetime earnings result in higher benefits. If there were some years when you did not work or had low earnings, your benefit amount may be lower than if you had worked steadily.

Your benefit payment also is affected by the age at which you decide to retire. If you retire at age 62 (the earliest possible retirement age for Social Security), your benefit will be lower than if you wait until later to retire. This is explained in more detail below. **Note:** Each year, about three months before your birthday, you receive a Social Security Statement. It can be a valuable tool to help you plan a secure financial future. It provides you with a record of your earnings and gives estimates of what your Social Security benefits would be at different retirement ages. It also gives an estimate of the disability benefits you could receive if you become severely disabled before retirement, as well as estimates of the survivors benefits that Social Security would provide your spouse and eligible family members when you die.

Early Retirement

You can get Social Security retirement benefits as early as age 62, but if you retire before your full retirement age, your benefits will be permanently reduced, based on your age. For example, if you retire at age 62, your benefit would be about 20 percent lower than what it would be if you waited until you reach full retirement age.

Full Retirement Age

The "full retirement age" is 65 for people who were born before 1938. But because of longer life expectancies, the Social Security law was changed to gradually increase the full retirement age until it reaches age 67. This change affects people born in 1938 and later. Check the following table to find your full retirement age.

Age to Receive Full Social Security Benefits

Year of birth	Full retirement age
1937 or earlier	65
1938	65 and 2 months
1939	65 and 4 months
1940	65 and 6 months
1941	65 and 8 months
1942	65 and 10 months
1943–1954	66
1955	66 and 2 months
1956	66 and 4 months
1957	66 and 6 months
1958	66 and 8 months
1959	66 and 10 months
1960 and later	67

Note: People who were born on January 1 of any year should refer to the previous year.

Remember, no matter what your full retirement age is, you still will be able to retire at age 62 if you have earned enough Social Security credits, but your monthly benefits will be permanently reduced. Some people stop working before age 62. But if they do, the years with no earnings will probably mean a lower Social Security benefit when they retire.

Note: Sometimes health problems force people to retire early. If you cannot work because of health problems, you should consider applying for Social Security disability benefits. The amount of the disability benefit is the same as a full, unreduced retirement benefit. If you are receiving Social Security disability benefits when you reach full retirement age, those benefits will be converted to retirement benefits. For more information, call us to ask for a copy of the publication, *Disability Benefits* (Publication No. 05-10029).

Delayed Retirement

You may choose to keep working even beyond your full retirement age. If you do, you can increase your future Social Security benefits in two ways.

Each additional year you work adds another year of earnings to your Social Security record. Higher lifetime earnings may mean higher benefits when you retire. Also, your benefit will increase automatically by a certain percentage from the time you reach your full retirement age until you start receiving your benefits or until you reach age 70. The percentage varies depending on your year of birth. For example, if you were born in 1943 or later, we will add 8 percent per year to your benefit for each year that you delay signing up for Social Security beyond your full retirement age.

Note: If you decide to delay your retirement, *be sure to sign up for Medicare at age 65*. In some circumstances, medical insurance costs more if you delay applying for it.

Deciding When to Retire

Choosing when to retire is an important but personal decision. Regardless of the age you choose to retire, it is a good idea to contact Social Security in advance to see which month is best to claim benefits. In some cases, your choice of a retirement month could mean higher benefit payments for you and your family.

In deciding when to retire, it is important to remember that financial experts say you will need 70–80 percent of your preretirement income to have a comfortable retirement. Since Social Security replaces only about 40 percent of preretirement income for the average worker, it is important to have pensions, savings and investments.

It may be to your advantage to have your Social Security benefits start in January, even if you do not plan to retire until later in the year. Depending on your earnings and your benefit amount, it may be possible for you to start collecting benefits even though you continue to work. Under current rules, many people can receive the most benefits possible with an application that is effective in January.

In some cases, it may be to your advantage to apply for benefits three months before the date you want your benefits to start. Because the rules can be complicated, we urge you to discuss your plans with a Social Security claims representative in the year before the year you plan to retire.

Retirement Benefits

For Widows and Widowers

Widows and widowers can begin receiving Social Security benefits at age 60, or at age 50 if they are disabled. And they can take a reduced benefit on one record and later switch to a full benefit on the other record. For example, a woman could take a reduced widow's benefit at 60 or 62 and then switch to her full (100 percent) retirement benefit when she reaches full retirement age. The rules vary depending on the situation, so you should talk to a Social Security representative about the options available to you.

For Family Members
If you are getting Social Security retirement benefits, some members of your family also can receive benefits. Those who can include:

- Wives or husbands, if they are age 62 or older;
- Wives or husbands who are younger than 62, if they are taking care of their child entitled on your record who is under age 16 or disabled;
- Former wives or husbands, if they are age 62 or older (see "Benefits for a divorced spouse");
- Children up to age 18 or 19, if they are full-time students who have not yet graduated from high school; and
- Disabled children, even if they are age 18 or older.

If you become the parent of a child (including an adopted child) after you begin receiving benefits, let us know about the child so we can decide if the child is eligible for benefits.

Note: Children's benefits are available only to unmarried children. However, in certain situations, benefits are payable to a disabled child who marries someone who is also eligible as a disabled child.

For Spouses
A spouse who has not worked or who has low earnings can be entitled to as much as one-half of the retired worker's full benefit. If you are eligible for both your own retirement benefits and for benefits as a spouse, we always pay your own benefits first. If your benefits as a spouse are higher than your retirement benefits, you will get a combination of benefits equaling the higher spouse benefit.

If spouses want to get Social Security retirement benefits before they reach full retirement age, the amount of the benefit is reduced permanently. The amount of reduction depends on when the person reaches full retirement age.

For example:

- If full retirement age is 65, a spouse can get 37.5 percent of the worker's unreduced benefit at age 62;

- If full retirement age is 66, a spouse can get 35 percent of the worker's unreduced benefit at age 62;
- If full retirement age is 67, a spouse can get 32.5 percent of the worker's unreduced benefit at age 62.

The amount of the benefit increases at later ages up to the maximum of 50 percent at full retirement age. If full retirement age is other than those shown here, the amount of the benefit will fall between 32.5 percent and 37 percent at age 62.

However, if your spouse is taking care of a child who is under age 16 or who gets Social Security disability benefits, your spouse gets full benefits, regardless of age.

Here is an example:

Mary Ann qualifies for a retirement benefit of $250 and a spouse's benefit of $400. At her full retirement age, she will receive her own $250 retirement benefit, and we will add $150 from her spouse's benefit, for a total of $400. If she takes her retirement benefit before her full retirement age, both amounts will be reduced.

Note: Your current spouse cannot receive spouse's benefits until you file for retirement benefits.

Maximum Family Benefits

If you have children eligible for Social Security, each will receive up to one-half of your full benefit. But there is a limit to the amount of money that can be paid to a family—usually 150–180 percent of your own benefit payment. If the total benefits due to your spouse and children are more than this limit, their benefits will be reduced. Your benefit will not be affected.

For a Divorced Spouse

Your divorced spouse can get benefits on your Social Security record if the marriage lasted at least 10 years. Your divorced spouse must be 62 or older and unmarried. The amount of benefits he or she gets has no effect on the amount of benefits you or your current spouse can get.

Also, if you and your ex-spouse have been divorced for at least two years and you and your ex-spouse are at least 62, he or she can get benefits even if you are not retired.

How to Sign Up for Social Security

You can apply for retirement benefits online at *www.socialsecurity.gov*, or you can call our toll-free number, 1-800-772-1213. Or you can make an appointment to visit any Social Security office to apply in person.

Depending on your circumstances, you will need some or all of the documents listed below. But do not delay applying for benefits because you do not have all the information. If you do not have a document you need, we can help you get it.

Information Needed

- Your Social Security number
- Your birth certificate
- Your W-2 forms or self-employment tax return for last year
- Your military discharge papers if you had military service
- Your spouse's birth certificate and Social Security number if he or she is applying for benefits
- Children's birth certificates and Social Security numbers, if you are applying for children's benefits
- Proof of U.S. citizenship or lawful alien status if you (or a spouse or child applying for benefits) were not born in the United States
- The name of your bank and your account number so your benefits can be deposited directly into your account.

You will need to submit original documents or copies certified by the issuing office. You can mail or bring them to Social Security. We will make photocopies and return your originals.

Your Right to Appeal Documents

If you disagree with a decision made on your claim, you can appeal it. The steps you can take are explained in the publication *The Appeals Process* (Publication No. 05-10041), which is available from Social Security.

You have the right to be represented by an attorney or other qualified person of your choice. More information is in the publication *Your Right to Representation* (Publication No. 05-10075), which also is available from Social Security.

If You Work and Get Benefits

You can continue to work and still receive retirement benefits. Your earnings in (or after) the month you reach your full retirement age will not reduce your Social Security benefits. However, your benefits will be reduced if your earnings exceed certain limits for the months before you reach your full retirement age.

Here is how it works:

If you are younger than full retirement age, $1 in benefits will be deducted for each $2 in earnings you have above the annual limit.

In the year you reach your full retirement age, your benefits will be reduced $1 for every $3 you earn over an annual limit until the month you reach full retirement age. Once you reach full retirement age, you can keep working and earn all you can, and your Social Security benefit will not be reduced.

If, during the year, your earnings are higher or lower than you estimated, let us know as soon as possible so we can adjust your benefits. If you want more information on how earnings affect your retirement benefit, call us for a copy of the publication, *How Work Affects Your Benefits* (Publication No. 05-10069), which has current annual and monthly earnings limits.

A Special Monthly Rule

A special rule applies to your earnings for one year, usually your first year of retirement. Under this rule, you can receive a full Social Security check for any month you are "retired," regardless of your yearly earnings. Your earnings must be under a monthly limit. If you are self-employed, the work you do in your business is taken into consideration as well.

If you want more information on how earnings affect your retirement benefit, call us for a copy of the publication, *How Work Affects Your Benefits* (Publication No. 05-10069), which has current annual and monthly earnings limits.

Your Benefits May Be Taxable

About one-third of people who get Social Security have to pay income taxes on their benefits.

- If you file a federal tax return as an "individual," and your combined income* is between $25,000 and $34,000, you may have to pay taxes on 50 percent of your Social Security benefits. If your combined income is more than $34,000, up to 85 percent of your Social Security benefits is subject to income tax.
- If you file a joint return, you may have to pay taxes on 50 percent of your benefits if you and your spouse have a combined income* that is between $32,000 and $44,000. If your combined income* is more than $44,000, up to 85 percent of your Social Security benefits is subject to income tax.
- If you are married and file a separate return, you probably will pay taxes on your benefits.

At the end of each year, we will mail you a Social Security Benefit Statement (Form SSA-1099) showing the amount of

---

*On the 1040 tax return, your "combined income" is the sum of your adjusted gross income plus nontaxable interest plus one-half of your Social Security benefits.

benefits you received. You can use this statement when you are completing your federal income tax return to find out if you have to pay taxes on any of your benefits.

Although you are not required to have federal taxes withheld, you may find it easier than paying quarterly estimated tax payments.

For more information, call the Internal Revenue Service's toll-free telephone number, 1-800-829-3676, to ask for Publication 554, Tax Information for Older Americans, and Publication 915, Social Security Benefits and Equivalent Railroad Retirement Benefits.

Pensions from Work Not Covered by Social Security

If you get a pension from work where you paid Social Security taxes, that pension will not affect your Social Security benefits. However, if you get a pension from work that was not covered by Social Security—for example, the federal civil service, some state or local government employment or work in a foreign country—your Social Security benefit may be reduced.

For more information, call Social Security to ask for the publications *Government Pension Offset*—for government workers who may be eligible for Social Security benefits on the earnings record of a husband or wife (Publication No. 05-10007); and *Windfall Elimination Provision*—for people who worked in another country or government workers who also are eligible for their own Social Security benefits (Publication No. 05-10045).

Leaving the United States

If you are a U.S. citizen, you can travel or live in most foreign countries without affecting your eligibility for Social Security benefits. However, there are a few countries—Cambodia, Cuba, North Korea, Vietnam and many of the former Soviet Union republics (except Armenia, Estonia, Latvia, Lithuania and Russia)—where we cannot send Social Security checks.

If you work outside the United States, different rules apply in determining if you can get benefits. For more information, call us to ask for a copy of the publication, *Your Payments While You Are Outside the United States* (Publication No. 05-10137).

Medicare

The following material is a continuation from the U.S. government Medicare site:

Medicare is a national health insurance plan for people who are 65 or older. (Although the full retirement age for Social Security benefits is increasing, the age to qualify for Medicare remains 65.) People who are disabled or have permanent kidney failure can get Medicare if they are younger than 65.

Medicare has two parts—hospital insurance and medical insurance. Most people have both parts. Hospital insurance, sometimes called Part A, covers inpatient hospital care and certain follow-up care. You already have paid for it as part of your Social Security taxes while you were working. Medical insurance, sometimes called Part B, pays for physicians' services and some other services not covered by hospital insurance. Medical insurance is optional, and you must pay monthly premiums.

If you are already getting Social Security benefits when you turn 65, your Medicare starts automatically. If you are not getting Social Security, you should sign up for Medicare before your 65th birthday, even if you are not ready to retire. For more information, call us to ask for the publication, *Medicare* (Publication No. 05-10043).

Help for Low-Income Medicare Beneficiaries

If you have a low income and few resources, your state may pay your Medicare premiums and, in some cases, other "out-of-pocket" Medicare expenses, such as deductibles and coinsurance.

Funding Your Retirement

Only your state can decide whether you qualify for help under this program. If you think you qualify, contact your state or local medical assistance (Medicaid) agency, social services, or welfare office. You can get more information about this program from the publication, *Medicare Savings Programs*. To get a copy, call the Medicare toll-free number, 1-800-MEDICARE (1-800-633-4227, or visit *www.medicare.gov* and click on Publications.

Medicare beneficiaries whose income is too high to qualify for low-income subsidies can sign up for the new prescription drug plan (Part D). Commonwealth Fund has made a study which estimates that, in the first year under the standard drug benefit, 38 percent of enrollees will be subject to the no-coverage gap, and another 14 percent will exceed the threshold of catastrophic coverage.

Your IRA

What Not to Do with Your IRA

If you cash out a retirement savings account before you reach the age of $59^1/_2$ it can become very expensive for you. The plan administrator is required to withhold 20 percent of your account balance for tax purposes and you will also have to pay a tax on what you withdraw as well as a 10 percent penalty.

What You Must Do with Your IRA

You must start taking distribution from your retirement savings account April 1 of the year following the year in which you turn $70^1/_2$. Generally it is a mistake to wait until this time as you will have to take two distributions in that year. Take the distribution earlier and you separate the distributions into two tax years, which will usually lower your income and thus your tax bill in each year.

You need not take your distribution in cash. If you own a stock you wish to keep take your distribution in shares equal to the value of your required distribution and pay the income tax on the stock value. This stock can be deposited in a taxable account for use as you wish.

Consider increasing your contributions to make sure you have enough money saved in your 401(k), or IRA to be able to retire.

There is a catch-up provision that allows seniors 50 and older to put additional funds in their retirement accounts. In 2005, for example you can put an additional $4,000 in your 401(k), and those go up $1,000 in 2006. You can put $500 additional in your IRA, and this goes up to $1,000 in 2006.

The following information with respect to Social Security should help you calculate your benefits and make financial plans for your retirement. In 2004 according to the Social Security Administration:

1. The average life expectancy was $82^1/_2$.
2. The average monthly benefit was $922.
3. The maximum taxable earnings for Social Security was $87,900.

Questions and Answers to Help with Your Calculations and Planning

The National Committee to Preserve Social Security & Medicare has a Web site where you can ask questions. Go to *http://www.ncpssm.org/contact/ask/* and e-mail questions. Here are some typical questions and answers:

Q: Should I start getting my Social Security benefits at 62, or should I wait until my full retirement age?

A: There is no absolutely correct answer to this question. But as a rule of thumb if you are sick or in poor health you should probably ask for your benefits at 62.

If you are in good health it usually better to wait until your full retirement time. Full retirement age will move upwards over the coming years, and the reductions for taking earlier benefits will increase. Right now payments are reduced by

24 percent for a 62-year-old who elects to take early retirement. By 2022 this amount is expected to be 30 percent less than at full retirement age. According to the Social Security Administration in 2002, 56 percent of new retirees elected to take their benefits as they became eligible to do so.

Conclusion: If you expect to live a long life you should not take Social Security benefits until you are 65. Also taking benefits early will not only lessen the amount of your check while you are alive, but will affect your widowed spouse as well. If you are in poor health or if taking Social Security early means taking less from tax-deferred accounts like IRAs or 401(k)s you should give strong consideration toward doing so.

Other Sources

Check how your retirement withdrawal strategy would have fared historically: *http://www.early-retirement.org/*.

Income comparison (geographic): Compare what your income will buy from city to city. Go to *http://www.bestplaces.net/default.aspx*, and type your income into the Cost of living link.

The American Savings Education Council offers a handy way to figure out how much money you will need to retire comfortably: *http://www.asec.org/ballpark/*.

Check how much money you will need to retire using the Retirement Probability Analyzer. This is a complicated but valuable tool from the Society of Actuaries Web site: *http://www.soa.org/ccm/content/*.

Wills

Most seniors with an estate of value already have an attorney and have prepared a will to distribute their assets according to their wishes and the laws of the state in which they have legal residence. For those of you who have not executed such a document you can access information to do it without an attorney. However I would urge you to consult an attorney even after you have prepared your own will. This will avoid problems that you could not possibly have anticipated as a layperson.

Nolo provides excellent will-making software: Quicken® WillMaker Plus 2006. Go to *http://referral.nolo.com/nc.cfm?t=EF0004BA003703* or go to *http://www.nolo.com/* and click on Wills & Estate Planning. You will also find retirement planning and elder care legal information on 401(k) plans, Roth IRAs, assisted living, nursing homes, Social Security benefits, and more.

Information on Taxes

Some seniors do not need to file a return.

You *may* not have to file a tax return if you were 65 or older on January 1, as long as you don't trip the income trigger as explained below. However, it is always a good idea to double check with your accountant or the IRS as rules change from time to time.

The Internal Revenue Service says you must file a return if you are single and you have income of more than $8,950 not counting Social Security income, or if you are the head of a household and your income is more than $11,200 not counting Social Security income.

This also applies to individuals who are married and filing jointly and either you or your spouse is 65 or older and you have income of more than $16,550 not counting Social Security income. Lastly if you are married and filing jointly and both you and your spouse are 65 or older and have a combined income of at least $17,500 not counting Social Security income.

Even if your income is below these limits, if you had taxes withheld from your income, you should file to get a refund of taxes that were withheld.

If you have to file a return because you are 65 or older, you can claim a higher standard deduction. This deduction is

$5,900 if you file as a single. If you are over 65, are married, and are filing a joint return and your spouse is not 65, then the deduction is $10,450.

If both of you are 65 or older and married and filing a joint return, and you are claiming your spouse's exemption, the standard deduction is $11,400.

Additionally seniors can count qualified home nursing care and long-term insurance care premiums when doing your tax returns, as these are considered medical expenses. To deduct medical expenses, the amount spent has to be more than 7.5 percent of your adjusted gross income.

If you are elderly, live with a child, and are paying for more than half of the child's living expenses, you may be able to claim the child as a dependent. In addition, children may be able to claim their parents as dependents even if they do not live in the same home, as long you are paying more than half of your parent's total support for the year.

If this sounds confusing you should check with a tax accountant or Social Security before you make a decision on whether or not to file.

The Web site *http://www.taxmama.com/* is a helpful place to visit for anyone seeking guidance on income tax issues or, heaven forbid, income tax problems.

Trusts

Retirement planning often involves various types of trusts. You should talk with your attorney to see if one or more of these trusts are appropriate for you.

Credit Shelter Trust

Ensures that the Estate Tax Exemption Amounts of both spouses are applied to the estate.

Charitable Remainder Trust

Can convert your appreciated assets into a lifetime income source without incurring capital gains or estate taxes. One or more charities will benefit from your donation.

QTIP Trust (Qualified Terminal Interest Property)
Allows for the deceased spouse to provide an ongoing income for the surviving spouse. The deceased spouse in this case designates beneficiaries for the remaining assets in the event of the surviving spouse's death.

Marital Trust
Provides for payment of all its assets to the surviving spouse. When the surviving spouse passes, the assets of the marital trust are included in his/her gross estate.

Confused? This is the best reason to see your attorney and have these trusts properly explained to you. Most trusts are designed to save on taxes and carry out wishes after death.

15

Estate Planning

Chapter Overview

- Finding an Attorney
- "Do Not Resuscitate" Forms/Advance Directives
- Funeral Needs and Health Care
- Personal Information Form

I could have written an entire book on estate planning. In fact, there are many such books currently on the market, and your attorney, financial advisor, estate planner, accountant, etc., can provide you with a great deal more information than is covered in this short chapter. I have just chosen to cover a few of the subjects that seem to be at the forefront of seniors' concerns right now.

Finding an Attorney

To reach a list of attorneys specializing in estate planning, go to the American College of Trust and Estate Counsel's Web site, *http://www.actec.org/public/roster/search.asp*.

The American Bar Association Web site, *http://www.abanet.org/rppt/public/home.html*, offers the following advice:

> When asked, "Should I give a member of my family a power of attorney?" the following answer is provided: "There is no easy answer to this question. You could be creating a difficult situation for your family and heirs. You could also be solving a number of problems. Your attorney should be able to give you guidelines to follow however it is usually best to get your children and heirs to approve these plans ahead of time. However it is important to 'spell out' what you want ahead of time. This approach generally avoids at least some of problems (and suits) that could result. Remember the power of attorney covers your finances but you also need a document that covers your health care decisions if you are unable to act for yourself. A medical power of attorney can help, but each state has different laws and regulations governing what can and can't be done.

"Do Not Resuscitate" Forms/Advance Directives

Many people across the United States have become aware of what a "Do Not Resuscitate" (DNR) form is after reading the sad story of a young woman in Florida whose physicians declared essentially brain dead. Her husband wanted to disconnect her from life support as her prognosis for recovery was virtually nonexistent, but her parents wanted to keep her alive using life support. The State of Florida also became involved in this sad case, which would not have come to this conclusion had she signed a DNR prior to her unfortunate accident.

If you wish to download a DNR form you may do so from either of the sites listed below. However, it is in your best interest to also check with an attorney with regard to your particular state's laws. Many people also include some kind of letter to loved ones along with this form telling of their wishes and indicating that they know how hard this decision will be should this time ever come. This letter will make it a little easier for a loved one to instruct the physician to turn off life support.

Forms and Information

http://www.ochealthinfo.com/docs/forms/ems_dnr_form.pdf

http://www.med.umich.edu/1libr/aha/umlegal03.htm

Funeral Needs and Health Care

Most retirement plans put too much emphasis on money issues and don't focus enough on the need to manage healthcare and funeral needs in a way that keeps retirees in control when ill health and other problems arise.

The Web site *http://www.finalplanning.info/* provides information to help seniors manage and solve the many problems created by insurance and Medicare rules, regulations, eligibility, and so on, as far as health care is concerned. This excellent resource also gives assistance in arranging a funeral without getting victimized and includes a funeral buyer's guide and much, much more.

The site also offers interactive planners that boil down complex issues into simple language, prompting retirees to state their preferences in a document that can be filed with personal papers for later use.

If you are worried that you could be unable to make informed decisions because of some debilitating illness or stroke, you can avoid this terrible predicament by executing a living will or health-care directive and a medical power of attorney for health care. These documents will ensure that important decisions will be in the hands of those who you so designate. The person you choose should be someone you trust absolutely, perhaps a member of your family, a close friend, or attorney. Remember that the person you choose may have to fight with others who do not agree with your directives, so pick someone who is strong enough to fight for your wishes. Choose someone who lives near to you as it is possible that this individual might have to spend a good deal of time supervising the medical decisions that are being made, and traveling from a distance could prove extremely difficult.

It is also a good idea to execute a durable power of attorney for finances to manage your finances in case you are unable to act. Once again, choose someone who is knowledgeable in this area, who lives nearby, and who is strong enough to fight for your directives. This person must also understand your health-care wishes to avoid any possibilities of a conflict.

The American Bar Association (ABA) Web site is an excellent resource. Here is an outline of the information this site provides at *http://www.abanet.org/rppt/public/home.html*.

Estate Planning Overview
   What Is Estate Planning?

An Introduction to Wills
   What Happens If You Die without a Will?
   What a Will Does
   What a Will Does Not Do
   How to Execute a Will

Types of Non-Probate Property
Jointly Owned Property
Trusts
Annuities and Retirement Benefits
Life Insurance

Revocable Trusts
What Is a Revocable Living Trust?

Power-of-Attorney
Introduction
Who Should Be Your Agent?
How the Agent Should Sign
Beyond Signing Checks
State Laws Vary
What If I Move?
Will My Power of Attorney Expire?

Living Wills, Health-Care Proxies, and Advance Health-Care Directives
Introduction
Living Wills
Health-Care Proxy
Why Have Health Directives?
Obtaining and Maintaining Living Wills and Health-Care Proxies
Organ and Tissue Donation
Communication Is the Key

Other Resources on Living Wills

The Probate Process
What Is Probate?
Should You Avoid Probate?

Planning with Retirement Benefits
Income Taxation of Qualified Plans and IRAs
Distribution of Plan Assets to the Participant
Distribution of Plan Assets after the Participant's Death
Estate Tax Considerations
Planning Considerations

Guidelines for Individual Executors and Trustees
Introduction
Understanding the Will
Is Probate Necessary?
Managing Estate Assets
Handling Debts and Expenses
Funding the Bequests
Trust Administration
Closing the Estate
Common Questions

The Lawyer's Role
What Is the Lawyer's Role?

Who We Are
About the Section of Real Property, Probate, and Trust Law

Tax Changes from 2001
Changes to Federal Estate Taxes 2004–2010

If filled out properly, the form below can save your spouse and family countless hours of searching for information and the distress of trying to find information that may even not exist. It will also give you the opportunity to reflect on some of your possessions as well as locate documents and information that you might not have even thought about for some time. It is strongly suggested that you fill out this form and give a copy to your spouse to fill out as well.

Personal Information Form

Complete and leave a copy with your will, with your attorney, your spouse, or your caretaker.

Updated _____

Name _____ Address _____
SS # _____ City _____
e-mail _____ State ___ Zip _____
Phone _____
Cell phone _____

Spouse _____
SS # _____
e-mail _____
Cell phone _____

Attorney _____
Phone _____ FAX _____
Cell phone _____ e-mail _____

Accountant _____
Phone _____ FAX _____
Cell phone _____ e-mail _____

Stockbroker _____
Phone _____ FAX _____
Cell phone _____ e-mail _____

Financial Planner _____
Phone _____ FAX _____
Cell phone _____ e-mail _____

Passwords
Computer _____ Internet Provider _____
DSL/Cable Connection _____ e-mail _____
Other Passwords _____

IN THIS SECTION

Children/grandchildren/people in your will

Name _____
Phone _____ Cell Phone _____
FAX _____
e-mail _____

Name _____
Phone _____ Cell Phone _____
FAX _____
e-mail _____

Name _____
Phone _____ Cell Phone _____
FAX _____
e-mail _____

Executors & Trustees

Name _____
Phone _____ Cell Phone _____
FAX _____
e-mail _____

Name _____
Phone _____ Cell Phone _____
FAX _____
e-mail _____

Name _____
Phone _____ Cell Phone _____
FAX _____
e-mail _____

Estate Planning

From this point on, allow space within entries for whatever is applicable: phone, cell phone, fax, e-mail, account numbers, descriptions, company names, persons' names, key numbers, safe deposit numbers, expiration dates.

Medical

Physicians

Name _____ Specialty _____
Phone _____

Name _____ Specialty _____
Phone _____

Name _____ Specialty _____
Phone _____

Dentist

Name _____ Phone _____

Veterinary

Name _____ Phone _____
(give name, breed, color, birth date, date annual shots due, habits—i.e. indoor or outdoor—for each pet)

Medical—Insurance
Medicare pending _____
Medicare (spouse) pending _____

Long-Term Health Care
Policy Number _____ Company _____
Agent _____ Phone number _____

Financial

Banks

Name _____ Location _____
Checking Account # _____
Savings Account # _____

Name _____ Location _____
Checking Account # _____
Savings Account # _____

Mortgage Information
Name of holder _____ Account # _____
Amount paid monthly _____
Address _____
Phone number _____

Name of holder _____ Account # _____
Amount paid monthly _____
Address _____
Phone number _____

Brokerages
Name of Firm _____
Name of Broker _____
Account Number _____
Federal Taxes Due dates _____ Amounts _____
State Taxes Due dates _____ Amounts _____
Real Estate Taxes Property Address _____
Due dates _____ Amounts _____
Real Estate Taxes Property Address _____
Due dates _____ Amounts _____

Social Security
Amount Received _____ By Check _____
By Direct Deposit _____
Pension Name of Provider _____
Amount Received _____ Due date _____

Life Insurance Policies
Name of Agent _____
Phone Number _____ Policy Number _____
Insurance Company _____
Amount of Policy _____

Estate Planning

Name of Agent _____
Phone Number _____ Policy Number _____
Insurance Company _____
Amount of Policy _____

Auto Insurance Policies

Name of Agent _____
Phone Number _____ Policy Number _____
Insurance Company _____
Amount of Policy _____

Liability Insurance Policies

Name of Agent _____
Phone Number _____ Policy Number _____
Insurance Company _____
Amount of Policy _____

Home Insurance Policies

Name of Agent _____
Phone Number _____ Policy Number _____
Insurance Company _____
Amount of Policy _____

Other Insurance

Name of Agent _____
Phone Number _____ Policy Number _____
Insurance Company _____
Amount of Policy _____

Safe Deposit Box

Name of Bank _____
Location of Key & Other Information _____

Credit Cards

Name on card (primary card holder) _____
Card number _____
Identification secret word (like mother's maiden name, etc.)
_____
Drivers license number _____

Household
Utilities
Electric Company phone number _____
Gas Company phone number _____
Contractor that services heating/air conditioning
Name _____ Phone number _____
Plumber Name _____ Phone number _____
Landscaper/Gardener
Name of company _____ Phone number _____
Snow Removal Company _____
Phone number _____
Sanitation Company _____
Phone number _____
Home telephone numbers _____ & _____
Name of company _____ Phone number _____
Cell Phones _____ & _____
Name of company _____ Phone number _____
Cable or satellite provider _____
Phone number _____
News Delivery Service Phone Number _____
E-Z pass number _____ How is it paid for _____
Real estate agent _____ Phone number _____
Automobiles
1 _____ Dealership for service _____
Phone number _____
2 _____ Dealership for service _____
Phone number _____
Emergency
Family (to call in emergency)
Name _____ Phone number _____
Name _____ Phone number _____
Name _____ Phone number _____
Neighbors (to call in emergency)
Name _____ Phone number _____
Name _____ Phone number _____
Name _____ Phone number _____

Estate Planning   189

Housekeepers/aides/assistants
Name _____ Phone number _____
Position _____ SS# _____
Name _____ Phone number _____
Position _____ SS# _____
Alumni (who to contact)
Name _____ Phone number _____
Affiliation (college, high school, etc) _____

Location of documents and information
Insurance Policy Information

Kind of insurance (life, auto, home owners, liability, etc.)
_____
Name of company _____ Name of agent _____
Phone _____Company _____
Address _____
Policy # _____ Location of policy _____

Kind of insurance (life, auto, home owners, liability, etc.)
_____
Name of company _____ Name of agent _____
Phone _____Company _____
Address _____
Policy # _____ Location of policy _____

Kind of insurance (life, auto, home owners, liability, etc.)
_____
Name of company _____ Name of agent _____
Phone _____Company _____
Address _____
Policy # _____ Location of policy _____

Kind of insurance (life, auto, home owners, liability, etc.)
_____
Name of company _____ Name of agent _____
Phone _____Company _____
Address _____
Policy # _____ Location of policy _____

Kind of insurance (life, auto, home owners, liability, etc.)
_____

Name of company _____ Name of agent _____
Phone _____ Company _____
Address _____
Policy # _____ Location of policy _____

Kind of insurance (life, auto, home owners, liability, etc.)
_____

Name of company _____ Name of agent _____
Phone _____ Company _____
Address _____
Policy # _____ Location of policy _____

Financial Information
Location of wills & documents _____
Location of deeds, surveys, moneys spent on improvements
_____

Tax Information (current and prior years)
Location _____

Stock Certificates
Location _____

Automobile Title, Registration
Location _____

Home/Condo Purchase information
Location _____

16

When Friends Pass On

Chapter Overview

- List of Charities for Donations
- Poems to Send in a Condolence Card

List of Charities for Donations
Friends who wish to express concern beyond flowers, calls, and cards can be directed to *http://www.whatgoesaround.org/* (click on memorial give list), which provides a "give list" of charities to which you can donate.

Poems to Send in a Condolence Card
When a friend or loved one passes it is particularly difficult to show how much that person meant to you. *Gone from My Sight* beautifully expresses feelings, and I have sent this beautiful thought to many friends and loved ones who have lost someone close. In every case it was very much appreciated. I've also included a couple of my other favorites.

Gone from My Sight
by Henry Van Dyke

I am standing upon the sea-shore.
A ship at my side spreads its white sails to the morning breeze and starts for the blue ocean. It is an object of beauty and strength, and I stand and watch it until at length it hangs like a speck of white cloud just where the sea and the sky come down to mingle with each other.
Then someone at my side says
"There! She's gone."
Gone where? Gone from my sight—that is all.
She is just as large in mast and hull and spar as she was when she left my side and just as able to bear her load of living freight to her place of destination.
Her diminished size is in me—not in her; and just at the moment when someone at my side says
"There, she's gone."
There are other eyes watching and other voices ready to take up the glad shout.
"There she comes!"

A Woman's Last Word
By Robert Browning

Let's contend no more, Love,
Strive nor weep:
All be as before, Love,
—Only sleep!

What so wild as words are?
I and thou
In debate, as birds are,
Hawk on bough!

See the creature stalking
While we speak!
Hush and hide the talking,
Cheek on cheek!

What so false as truth is,
False to thee?
Where the serpent's tooth is
Shun the tree—

Where the apple reddens
Never pry—
Lest we lose our Edens,
Eve and I.

Be a god and hold me
With a charm!
Be a man and fold me
With thine arm!

Teach me, only teach, Love
As I ought
I will speak thy speech, Love,

Think thy thought—
Meet, if thou require it,
Both demands,
Laying flesh and spirit
In thy hands.
That shall be to-morrow
Not to-night:
I must bury sorrow
Out of sight:

—Must a little weep, Love,
(Foolish me!)
And so fall asleep, Love,
Loved by thee.

Kisses

The story goes that some time ago a man punished his 5-year-old daughter for wasting a roll of expensive gold wrapping paper. Money was tight and he became even more upset when the child pasted the gold paper so as to decorate a box to put under the Christmas tree.

Nevertheless, the little girl brought the gift box to her father the next morning and said, "This is for you, Daddy." The father was embarrassed by his earlier overreaction, but his anger flared again when he found the box was empty. He spoke to her in a harsh manner, "Don't you know, young lady, when you give someone a present there's supposed to be something inside the package?"

The little girl looked up at him with tears in her eyes and said, "Oh, Daddy, it's not empty. I blew kisses into it until it was full."

The father was crushed. He fell on his knees and put his arms around his little girl, and he begged her to forgive him for his unnecessary anger.

An accident took the life of the child only a short time later, and it is told that the father kept that gold box by his bed for all the years of his life.

Whenever he was discouraged or faced difficult problems he would open the box and take out an imaginary kiss and remember the love of the child who had put it there. Each of us has been given a golden box filled with love and kisses from our children, our family, our close friends, and also our special pets. There is no more precious possession anyone could ever hold.

Appendices

Overview

1. *The Coming of Fall in New England* by Larry Morse
2. Contact Information for Charities and Nonprofits
3. AARP's Best Employers for Workers over 50—Honorees for 2004
4. Dietary Guidelines for Americans, 2005
5. Estimates and Projections of the Older Population by Age Group, 1995–2010
6. List of Common Scams That Often Target Retirees
7. Publications of Help and Interest to Retirees and Seniors

   AARP Magazine *Modern Maturity*
   AARP the Magazine
   Aging
   50 Plus
   Good Life Magazine
   Kiplinger's Retirement Report
   Life Extension Magazine
   Money Magazine
   New Choices for Retirement Living
   Senior Journal
   Today's Senior
   USA Today
   The Wall Street Journal

Appendix 1

The Coming of Fall in New England
by Larry Morse

The first frost or two has mooned the area, but the damage is slight because the ground is so warm. This won't be the case long. October 5 or thereabouts is generally Crow Leaving Day and that's the Sign. Still the Silver Queen corn is in top form; there is no better corn than this. I will shortly gather the old fashioned apples—Golden Russets and the like—to take to the press. I shall make hard cider this year for the first time in a long time, and look forward to opening that first bottle next spring: Pull the cork—I like a sparkling hard cider—get some good cheese and crunchy bread and sit out in the March woodshed, protected from the bitter northwest wind, and turn your face to the sun. This is the right number.

I have pulled all the honey supers from the bees and put the organo-phosphate strips in to kill the varroa mites. I will have to spin this honey out soon and freeze it. It will be a dark-colored, dark-flavored honey, for goldenrod makes a very dark nectar, but some people prefer it to the lighter early honey. The white asters remain in full bloom and the bees are working them hard to fill the top brood box with honey for this winter. New England and wild asters are synonymous, the real New England, the one that doesn't exist any more except in these few backwater places. Hello New England, is this really you, the best companion of my life, the one who has never failed me? The real New England is the past master of the massed asters.

With the hard frosts, I will start feeding the bees sugar water—five pounds of sugar in a gallon of water and a teaspoon of Fumadil mixed in so the bees don't get diarrhea. Here, you have to feed the bees sugar water because they continue to fly with every warm day, long after the last flower is dead. If I do not give them sugar, they will begin to eat the stored honey that needs to be saved for true winter, and without which they will starve to death.

The bee yard is a pleasant place after the frosts as long as you don't get too close to the bees. Their disposition gets exceedingly touchy when the nectar and pollen are gone, and I have to wear the full bee suit when I put the sugar-water feeders in place, or I am dead meat. Nevertheless, the sun strikes in warmly in this protected place, and the memory of summer lingers and lingers, so I hang around and watch the bees gather in the hive doors to sun themselves. We are of the same mind, they and I, and we hold on to the old sweetness as long as may be. I don't know but what I shall put some rum in their sugar water. They take the water and pack it in empty cells in the upper box, and the thought pleases me that, with a little rum added, they are packing away a little toddy in glasses of the most perfect design.

Little by little, the cold will drive them indoors. They will seal all cracks and leaky crannies with propolis, and then they will put the queen in the middle and gather about her in a living, slowly moving ball. As the outside bees get cold, they will move inward, and the warm bees take up the outer shell. When they get hungry on one of the warmer days, they will move outward and dine on honey. One day, with a hard, slatey sky, perhaps, but the wind at last out of the southwest, they

The Coming of Fall in New England

will take the waxy tops off their little rum toddies and have a warm and comforting drink on the house, and who knows? Perhaps they will gather together again and dream of shining fields of dandelions and full nectar cells and long days of pollen and delight. This is a pleasant thought on the bitter days when I put my feet in my bunny slippers and get close to the wood stove. I have found that a glass of hot water, whose flat dull flavor has been qualified by a shot of John Jamieson, a slice of lemon and orange, a sprinkle of clove and a long stick of cinnamon cut from a tree on an amethyst island in a turquoise sea from which strange exotic fragrances stir in the swells—I say, I find that a glass of this and the wood stove remind me of the bees so that we have a warm drink together in our strange fellowship, and as they drift over the rafts of red clover, I walk dream trout streams, where the trout wait only for me and the wood peewee, deep in the hemlock forest, sings only for my ears.

Cold World people are very different from Warm World folks, and I have always thought this was genetic. When the cold weather comes, many—perhaps most—people start thinking about the Cayman Islands and wave-lapped shores, but other people, of which I am one, look north into the night and the cold. Next month, I would like to head north—should have the log cabin done by then and well stocked, fully prepared to spend the winter more or less alone. What a cheerful thought this is! To be fully set to run though the long brilliant nights on the snow machine, to spend the day ice fishing or moose hunting and the night dozing in the rocker by the old Glenwood.

I suspect we were separated one hundred thousand years ago, when the glaciers first crept south and swallowed the land. Some of our ancestors looked at the changing weather, listened to the cold rain slanting off the skin roof and watched the food flee before the coming winter, and they thought to themselves that they too had better move and right soon. But other ancestors learned how to store food, how to dress skins with the fur on, how to hide from the snow and cold, how to keep fires alive and well, so they stayed and, by the fire, learned how to speak and tell stories, how to live together in a small space, and to watch with delight as the stars on the crystal nights turned in their orbits. Here, in the Cold World, the Cold People lived and died; and I wouldn't be surprised to discover that it was here that we first learned to speak and the spirit waked for the first time.

Appendix 2

Contact Information for Charities and Nonprofits

The author and publisher made no attempt to verify the phone numbers or the legitimacy of the following charities and nonprofit organizations. This list is included for the reader's convenience only. A more complete list of charities and nonprofits can be found at *http://www.give.org/reports/index.asp*. Investigate before you volunteer or donate.

AARP Foundation • 202-434-2018

American Civil Liberties Foundation • 212-549-2500

American Foundation for AIDS Research • 800-392-6327

American Friends Service Committee • 800-638-8299

Alzheimer's Association • 800-272-3900

ALS Association—National Office • 888-949-2577

American Association of the Deaf-Blind • 301-495-4403

American Brain Tumor Association • 800-886-2282

American Cancer Society • 800-227-2345

American Diabetes Association • 800-342-2383

American Foundation for the Blind • 800-232-5463

American Heart Association • 800-242-8721

American Jewish Committee • 212-751-4000

American Kidney Fund • 215 241-7000
American Liver Foundation • 800-465-4837
American Lung Association • 212-315-8700
American Macular Degeneration Foundation • 888-622-8527
American Red Cross • 202-303-4498
Animal Rescue Foundation • 925-256-1273
Anti-Defamation League • 212-885-7700
Arthritis Foundation • 800-238-7800
American Society for the Prevention of Cruelty to Animals • 212-876-7700
Big Brothers/Big Sisters of America • 215-567-7000
Boys & Girls Clubs of America • 404-487-5700
Cancer Fund of America • 800-578-5284
Cancer Research & Prevention Foundation • 800-227-2732
CARE USA • 800-422-7385
Catholic Relief Services • 410-625-2220
Children's Defense Fund • 202-628-8787
City of Hope • 800-826-4673
Crohn's & Colitis Foundation of America • 800-932-2423
Cystic Fibrosis Foundation • 800-344-4823
Disabled American Veterans • 859-441-7300
Doctors Without Borders, USA • 888-392-0392
Easter Seals • 312-726-6200
Epilepsy Foundation • 800-470-1655
Feed the Children • 800-627-4556
Global Fund for Women • 415-202-7640
Greenpeace • 202-462-1177
Humane Society of the US • 202-452-1100
Juvenile Diabetes Research Foundation • 800-533-2873

Contact Information for Charities

Lance Armstrong Foundation • 512-236-8820
Leukemia & Lymphoma Society • 800-955-4572
Lupus Foundation of America—N.O. • 301-670-9292
Mothers Against Drunk Driving • 800-438-6233
March of Dimes Against Birth Defects • 888-663-4637
Medic Alert Foundation U.S. • 800-ID-ALERT
Multiple Sclerosis Foundation • 800-225-6495
Muscular Dystrophy Association • 800-572-1717
NAACP • 877-622-2798
National Alliance to End Homelessness • 202-638-1526
National Audubon Society • 212-979-3000
National Mental Health Association • 800-969-6642
National Police Defense Foundation • 888-723-3267
Oprah's Angel Network • 312-633-1000
Parkinson's Disease Foundation • 800-457-6676
Ronald McDonald House Charities • 630-623-7048
Salk Institute for Biological Studies • 858-453-4100
Salvation Army • 703-684-5500
Save The Children Federation • 800-243-5075
St. Jude Children's Research Hospital • 800-877-5833
United Cerebral Palsy Associations • 800-872-5827
United Jewish Communities • 212-284-6500
United Way of America • 800-892-2757
Veterans of Foreign Wars of the United States • 816-756-3390
Volunteer Match • 415-241-6868
Volunteers of America • 800-899-0089
Wilderness Society • 800-843-9453
World Society for the Protection of Animals • 508-879-8350
World Wildlife Fund • 202-293-4800

Appendix 3

AARP Best Employers for Workers over 50—Honorees for 2004

These companies and organizations, recognized by AARP for their best practices and policies for valuing the mature worker, are roadmaps for the workplaces of tomorrow. They recruit seniors for full-time as well as part-time and temporary positions.

Adecco Employment Services, Melville, NY
http://www.adeccousa.com/home.cfm
 A staffing and human resource solutions company that places temporary and full-time employees at client locations.

Beaumont Hospitals, Southfield, MI
http://www.beaumonthospitals.com/
 A provider of health-care services, medical education, and medical research.

Bon Secours Richmond Health System, Richmond, VA
http://www.bonsecours.com/
 A not-for-profit, multifacility health-care system with three hospitals and more than twenty-four outpatient service sites.

Brethren Village, Lancaster, PA
http://www.bv.org/

A not-for-profit continuing care retirement community offering choices and services to keep residents living independently for as long as possible.

Centegra Health System, Woodstock, IL
http://www.centegra.com/

A health-care system that includes several hospitals, the Centegra Primary Care physician network, a fitness center, and over twenty additional sites throughout its service area.

Deere & Company, Moline, IL
http://www.deere.com/

Manufactures, distributes, and finances a broad range of agricultural, construction, forestry, commercial, and consumer equipment.

Delaware North Companies Inc., Buffalo, NY
http://www.delawarenorth.com/

A hospitality and food service provider that provides visitor services at national parks and attractions, resorts, and at more than fifty sporting venues and thirty airports in the United States.

DentaQuest Ventures, Inc., Boston, MA
http://www.dentaquest.com/

National administrator of dental benefits.

First Horizon National Corporation, Memphis, TN
http://www.firsthorizon.com/

A nationwide financial services institution providing services to individuals and businesses.

Gemini, Incorporated, Cannon Falls, MN
http://www.signletters.com/

A manufacturer of metal and plastic letters for outdoor signage and customized, decorative metal plaques.

Hoffmann-La Roche Inc., Nutley, NJ
http://www.rocheusa.com/
An innovation-driven health-care company, with core businesses in pharmaceuticals and diagnostics.

Lee County Electric Cooperative, North Fort Myers, FL
http://www.lcec.net/
A not-for-profit electric distribution cooperative providing service and energy products to 165,000 customers in Southwest Florida.

Lincoln Financial Group, Philadelphia, PA
http://www.lfg.com/
Provides financial and security products to individuals and businesses.

Loudoun Healthcare, Inc., Leesburg, VA
http://www.loudounhealthcare.org/home/
A not-for-profit health-care organization providing a full continuum of quality health-care services.

Minnesota Life, St. Paul, MN
http://www.minnesotalife.com/
Provides insurance, pension, and investment products to more than six million clients in all fifty states and Puerto Rico.

Mitretek Systems, Falls Church, VA
http://www.mitretek.org/home.nsf
A nonprofit research and engineering company.

New York University Medical Center, New York, NY
http://med.nyu.edu
A not-for-profit health-care organization comprising the NYU Hospitals Center and the NYU School of Medicine.

North Memorial Health Care, Robbinsdale, MN
http://www.northmemorial.com/
A nonprofit health-care provider with more than eight hundred physicians and five thousand employees in its system.

Pitney Bowes, Inc., Stamford, CT
http://www.pitneybowes.com/
A provider of integrated mail and document management systems, services, and solutions.

Principal Financial Group, Des Moines, IA
http://www.principal.com/
Offers businesses, individuals, and institutional clients a wide range of financial products and services.

Scottsdale Healthcare, Scottsdale, AZ
http://www.shc.org/
A nonprofit health-care provider with two hospitals, outpatient centers, home health services, and a wide range of community outreach programs.

Scripps Health, San Diego, CA
http://www.scrippshealth.org/
A not-for-profit, community-based health-care system that includes five acute and tertiary care hospitals, numerous outpatient facilities, and home health-care services.

Smurfit-Stone Container Corporation, Clayton, MO
http://www.smurfit-stone.com/
A manufacturer of paperboard, paper-based packaging, and other packaging materials and paper-based products.

Sonoco, Hartsville, SC
http://www.sonoco.com/
A manufacturer of industrial and consumer packaging products and provider of packaging services.

SSM Health Care, St. Louis, MO
http://www.ssmhc.com/
A health-care network sponsored by the Franciscan Sisters of Mary that delivers patient care in the St. Louis region.

St. Mary's Medical Center, Huntington, WV
http://www.st-marys.org/
A regional medical center in the tri-state region of West Virginia, Ohio, and Kentucky, specializing in cardiac, oncology, trauma, and neuroscience services.

Stanley Consultants, Inc., Muscatine, IA
http://www.stanleyconsultants.com/
A multidisciplinary consulting firm that provides engineering, environmental, and construction services worldwide.

The Charles Stark Draper Laboratory, Inc. Cambridge, MA
http://www.draper.com/
A private, not-for-profit corporation engaged in applied research, engineering development, technology transfer, and advanced technical education.

The Methodist Hospital, Houston, TX
http://www.methodisthealth.com/
A nonprofit health-care organization made up of a flagship hospital, the Methodist Hospital, and three community hospitals.

The Vanguard Group, Valley Forge, PA
http://www.vanguard.com/
An investment management company that provides an array of financial products and services, including mutual fund investments and employer-sponsored retirement plan services.

Volkswagen of America, Inc., Auburn Hills, MI
http://www.vw.com/
Manufacturer of passenger cars and trucks.

WELBRO Building Corporation, Maitland, FL
http://www.welbro.com/
　A full-service construction management and general contracting company.

West Virginia University Hospitals, Morgantown, WV
http://health.wvu.edu/employment/
　A private, not-for-profit corporation that is closely tied to West Virginia University and includes three hospitals, a trauma center, and the WVU Eye Institute.

Westgate Resorts, Orlando, FL
http://www.westgateresorts.com/
　A privately held timeshare company that employs over five thousand people throughout the country.

Zurich North America, Schaumburg, IL
http://www.zurichna.com/
　A commercial property-casualty insurance provider serving the multinational, middle-market, and small business sectors in the United States and Canada

Appendix 4

Dietary Guidelines for Americans, 2005

Key Recommendations for the General Population

ADEQUATE NUTRIENTS WITHIN CALORIE NEEDS
Consume a variety of nutrient-dense foods and beverages within and among the basic food groups while choosing foods that limit the intake of saturated and *trans* fats, cholesterol, added sugars, salt, and alcohol.

Meet recommended intakes within energy needs by adopting a balanced eating pattern, such as the U.S. Department of Agriculture (USDA) Food Guide or the Dietary Approaches to Stop Hypertension (DASH) Eating Plan.

WEIGHT MANAGEMENT
To maintain body weight in a healthy range, balance calories from foods and beverages with calories expended.

To prevent gradual weight gain over time, make small decreases in food and beverage calories and increase physical activity.

PHYSICAL ACTIVITY
Engage in regular physical activity and reduce sedentary activities to promote health, psychological well-being, and a healthy body weight.

To reduce the risk of chronic disease in adulthood: Engage in at least 30 minutes of moderate-intensity physical activity, above usual activity, at work or home on most days of the week.

For most people, greater health benefits can be obtained by engaging in physical activity of more vigorous intensity or longer duration.

To help manage body weight and prevent gradual, unhealthy body weight gain in adulthood: Engage in approximately 60 minutes of moderate- to vigorous-intensity activity on most days of the week while not exceeding caloric intake requirements.

To sustain weight loss in adulthood: Participate in at least 60 to 90 minutes of daily moderate-intensity physical activity while not exceeding caloric intake requirements. Some people may need to consult with a health-care provider before participating in this level of activity.

Achieve physical fitness by including cardiovascular conditioning, stretching exercises for flexibility, and resistance exercises or calisthenics for muscle strength and endurance.

FOOD GROUPS TO ENCOURAGE

Consume a sufficient amount of fruits and vegetables while staying within energy needs. Two cups of fruit and 2½ cups of vegetables per day are recommended for a reference 2,000-calorie intake, with higher or lower amounts depending on the calorie level. Choose a variety of fruits and vegetables each day. In particular, select from all five vegetable subgroups (dark green, orange, legumes, starchy vegetables, and other vegetables) several times a week.

Consume 3 or more ounce-equivalents of whole-grain products per day, with the rest of the recommended grains coming from enriched or whole-grain products. In general, at least half the grains should come from whole grains.

Consume 3 cups per day of fat-free or low-fat milk or equivalent milk products.

FATS

Consume less than 10 percent of calories from saturated fatty acids and less than 300 mg/day of cholesterol, and keep *trans* fatty acid consumption as low as possible.

Keep total fat intake between 20 to 35 percent of calories, with most fats coming from sources of polyunsaturated and monounsaturated fatty acids, such as fish, nuts, and vegetable oils.

When selecting and preparing meat, poultry, dry beans, and milk or milk products, make choices that are lean, low-fat, or fat-free.

Limit intake of fats and oils high in saturated and/or *trans* fatty acids, and choose products low in such fats and oils.

CARBOHYDRATES

Choose fiber-rich fruits, vegetables, and whole grains often.

Choose and prepare foods and beverages with little added sugars or caloric sweeteners, such as amounts suggested by the USDA Food Guide and the DASH Eating Plan.

Reduce the incidence of dental caries by practicing good oral hygiene and consuming sugar- and starch-containing foods and beverages less frequently.

SODIUM AND POTASSIUM

Consume less than 2,300 mg (approximately 1 teaspoon of salt) of sodium per day.

Choose and prepare foods with little salt. At the same time, consume potassium-rich foods, such as fruits and vegetables.

ALCOHOLIC BEVERAGES

Those who choose to drink alcoholic beverages should do so sensibly and in moderation—defined as the consumption of up to one drink per day for women and up to two drinks per day for men.

Alcoholic beverages should not be consumed by some individuals, including those who cannot restrict their alcohol intake, women of childbearing age who may become pregnant, pregnant and lactating women, children and adolescents, individuals taking medications that can interact with alcohol, and those with specific medical conditions.

Alcoholic beverages should be avoided by individuals engaging in activities that require attention, skill, or coordination, such as driving or operating machinery.

FOOD SAFETY

To avoid microbial food-borne illness:

- Clean hands, food contact surfaces, and fruits and vegetables. Meat and poultry should not be washed or rinsed in areas of food preparation. Separate raw, cooked, and ready-to-eat foods while shopping, preparing, or storing foods.
- Cook foods to a safe temperature to kill microorganisms.
- Chill (refrigerate) perishable food promptly and defrost foods properly.
- Avoid raw (unpasteurized) milk or any products made from unpasteurized milk, raw or partially cooked eggs or foods containing raw eggs, raw or undercooked meat and poultry, unpasteurized juices, and raw sprouts.

Note: The Dietary Guidelines for Americans 2005 *contains additional recommendations for specific populations. The full document is available at* www.healthierus.gov/dietary guidelines.

Appendix 5

Estimates and Projections of the Older Population by Age Group: 1995-2010*

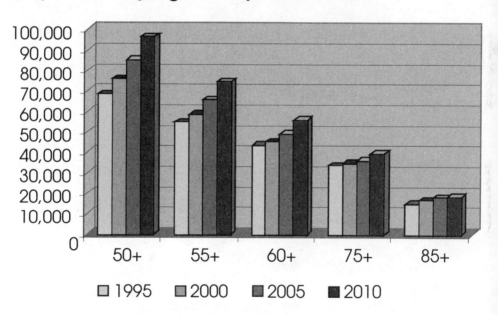

*Source: U.S. Bureau of the Census, Current Population Reports, P25-1130, "Population Projections of the United States, by Age, Sex, and Hispanic Origin: 1995 to 2050," February 1996; and "U.S. Population Estimates, by Age, Sex, Race, and Hispanic Origin: 1990 to 1994."

Labor Force Participation, Ages 55 to 64

	men	women
2002	69 percent	55 percent
2012	75 percent	64 percent

Source: *American Demographics* analysis of BLS data

65+ Labor Statistics**

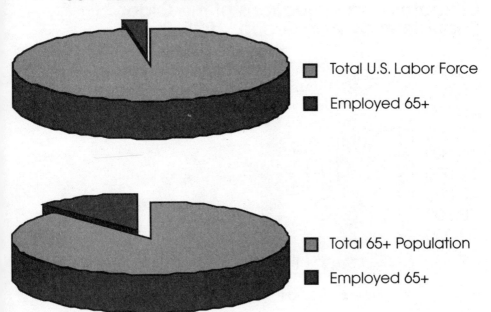

**Source: *A Profile of Older Americans* © 2004

Appendix 6

List of Common Scams That Often Target Retirees

- Guaranteed loan and credit offers that require an advance fee.
- Credit repair to insure you against stolen credit or credit cards. Also be wary of a Web site or caller that promises a free credit report and asks for your credit card number and or Social Security number. Any calls that purport to come from one of the three credit reporting agencies and solicits personal information is bogus.
- Phishing or contact by phone or e-mail purportedly from your bank, credit card company, or other service provider which asks you for information—in particular, your credit card PIN number. Legitimate firms never ask for this information by phone or e-mail.
- Lottery and sweepstakes offers or prize promotions in which you are told you have won money, vacations, travel, or other awards.
- Requests to aid a foreign government official or family member who will share moneys if you provide help, usually in the form of some seed money.
- Discount travel deals with upfront money from anyone other than a recognized, trusted travel agency or recognized hotel, airline, or cruise line.

Appendix 7

Publications of Help and Interest to Retirees and Seniors

AARP Magazine *Modern Maturity*

AARP the Magazine

Aging

50 Plus

Good Life Magazine

Kiplinger's Retirement Report

Life Extension Magazine

Money Magazine

New Choices for Retirement Living

Senior Journal

Today's Senior

USA Today

The Wall Street Journal

Index

A
AARP, 94
advance directives, 178–79, 180
age groups, percentage
  changes in, 8
Alzheimer's disease, 124,
  137–40
annuities, 154–55
assisted living, 20, 116–17

B
baby boomers, imminent
  retirement of, 7
Bench, Marcia, 15–17
BenefitsCheckUp, 109
BenefitsCheckUpRX, 109
Best, Samuel J., 2–3
Bland, Warren, 21
blueberries, 125–26
boredom, 2
brain, maintaining, 136
budgets, designing, 86

C
Canada
  buying prescription drugs
    from, 110–11
  moving to, 22
cancer, 129–31
*Career Coaching: An Insider's
  Guide* (Bench), 15

cats, 145–49
charitable remainder trust, 175
charities
  contact information for,
    33–36, 203–5
  for donations, 192
cities
  increase in population of,
    among seniors, 21
  most affordable, 22
clinical trials, 32–33
Clinton, Bill, 123
COBRA (Consolidated
  Omnibus Budget
  Reconciliation Act), 92
"The Coming of Fall in New
  England" (Morse), 199–202
computers
  for home office, 28
  instruction books for using, 83
  instructions on using, for
    seniors, 81–83
  primer for using, 63–81
  seniors' use of, 55
condolence card sentiments,
  192–96
continuing care communities,
  116
continuing-care facility, 20

costs of living, comparing among locales, 22
credit, protecting, 86–88
credit card fraud, 87
credit reports, 87–88
credit shelter trust, 175
Cropper, Carol Marie, 128
curry, 124–25

D
Dautrich, Kenneth, 2–3
DeBakey, Michael, 7
demographics, older age groups as percentage of population, 217
dietary guidelines, 123–24, 213–16
dogs, 142–45
Do Not Call Registry, 87
Do Not Resuscitate (DNR) forms, 178–79
Don't Retire, Rewire (Sedlar and Miners), 10
durable power of attorney, 180

E
education
  auditing classes, 38
  online schools, 38–49
  programs offered via online learning, 49–52
e-mail, instructions for, 55–63, 68–71
estate planning, 178
Evans, Richard, 109
expenditures, annual averages, for Americans, 23

F
faxes, for home office, 28
finances, protecting one's credit, 86–88
Food and Drug Administration, 32–33
Frey, William, 21
funeral needs, 179
furniture, for home office, 26

G
government retirement programs, 6

H
health care. *See also* Medicare
  employers saving on costs of, when hiring seniors, 10
  insurance premiums for, 90–91
  preparing for rising costs, 90–91
  spending on, 90
healthful eating, 122–23
health insurance, 8. *See also* Medicare
health reimbursement arrangements, 91
health savings accounts (HSA), 91
heart disease, 126–27
Heldrich Center for Workforce Development, 2–3
Hinterlong, J., 32
Home Equity Conversion Mortgage (HECM), 156
home equity, 155

home health care, 20, 117–18
home office, setting up, 25–30
hospice, 20–21
housing options, 20–21, 116–17

I
identity fraud, 86
income taxes, 174–75
  deducting medical expenses from, 105
Internet. *See also* Web sites
  literacy for seniors, 54
  uses for, 54
investments
  goals for, 156
  stocks vs. bonds, 157
IRA, 171–73

J
job search
  changes in methods, 15
  practical steps for, 11–13
  strategies for, 15–17

L
labor force participation, among seniors, 2–5
life expectancy, 7
lifestyle, factors affecting, 20
longevity, 122–23
long-term care insurance, 117–18

M
marital trust, 176
medical costs, increasing, 8
medical expenses, deducting from income tax, 105

medical power of attorney, 180
Medicare, 170–71
  drug discounts cards, 108–9
  Medicare Rights Center, 105
  Medicare Supplement Insurance, 91–92
  Part D, questions to consider, 104–5
  prescription drug coverage, 94–104
  rising premiums for, 8
memory loss, 134–35
Miners, Rick, 10–11
Morrow-Howell, N., 32
Morse, Larry, 22, 199–202
mortgages, 155–56
Moving Calculator, 22
My Life (Clinton), 123

N
New England, 22, 199–202
nonprofits, contact information for, 33–36, 203–5
nursing homes, 20, 116–17, 119
nutrition, 122
Nyberg, Alix, 90

O
older worker, defining, 5–6
ombudsmen, for housing options, 120

P
pensions, 6, 7, 158, 169
personal information form, 183–90
personal savings, 7–8

pets
  adopting, 149
  cats, 145–49
  dogs, 142–45
  losing, 1490
pharmacies
  online, 107
  shopping with, 109
prescription drugs
  buying from Canada, 110–11
  buying online, 107–9, 112–13
  consumer tips for purchasing, 111–12
  costs of, 90
  Guide to Medicare Prescription Drug Coverage, 94
  keeping track of, 105
  Medicare prescription drug coverage, 94–104
  price comparisons for, 108, 112
  tips for cost savings on, 106
publications, of help and interest to retirees and seniors, 221

Q
QTIP trust (qualified terminal interest property), 176

R
Rasbid, Diana, 55
résumés, 13–14, 16–17
retirement
  additional income needed for, 4
  age of, 154
  financial planning for, 6, 153–58
  redefining, 2–6
  traditional notion of, obsolete, 3–4
  work-filled, 3–6, 9
retirement community, 20
retirement income calculator, 158
retirement planner, 158
Retire in Style: 50 Affordable Places across America (Bland), 21
Retire Your Way (Bench), 15
reverse mortgages, 155–56
Rozario, P. A., 32
RVs, 22

S
Salary Comparison Calculator, 22
salary information, 15
saving money, 152–53
Savings Calculator, 154
scams, 87, 219
Sedlar, Jeri, 10–11
shredders, 28, 88
Social Security, 6, 7
  appeals to, 167
  retirement benefits, 163–66, 167–69
  retirement plan, 158–63
  signing up for, 166
states, increase in population of, among seniors, 21

T

Tang, F., 32
telephone, second line for home office, 28
temp agencies, 11
temporary assignments, 15
Thomas, Dave, 125
trusts, 175–76

V

Van Horn, Carl E., 2–3
volunteering
  benefits of, 32
  clinical trials, 32–33
  contact information for non-profits and charities, 33–36
  places for, 32

W

Web sites
  career coaching, 16
  clinical trials, 32–33
  cost of living comparisons, 22
  DNR forms, 179
  health and medicine, 127–29, 131–32
  helping in transition from full-time employment, 17
  housing options, 119–20
  insurance rating services, 117
  investments, 157
  job search, 12–13
  medication information, 113
  online pharmacies, 107, 113
  online schools, 38–49
  programs offered via online learning, 49–52
  résumé help, 13–14
  retirement finances, 158, 173, 180–82
  salary information, 15
  for volunteering, 32, 33–36
wills, 173–74
workforce
  demographic shifts in, 7
  participation in, for older age groups, 218
  reasons for seniors to return to, 7–9
  treatment of seniors in, 6, 9
workplace
  best employers for older workers, 18, 207–12
  characteristics of seniors in, 9–10
  hiring seniors, 2, 9–10
  jobs often filled by seniors, 14
  need for seniors in, 8
  questions for seniors to consider upon return to, 10–11
  returning to former employer, 15
  seniors' contribution to, 9–10
  treatment of seniors in, 6, 9

About the Author

Art Koff graduated from Dartmouth College in 1957 and did postgraduate work at the University of Chicago Executive Program. He started his career with the *Chicago Sun Times* and then spent thirty-one years with national and international advertising agencies.

After "retiring" Art helped develop and market one of the first automated job-posting systems, which was later acquired by a major player in the field. He also helped build a suite of over one thousand niche sites focused on recruiting. As a consultant and writer for the past nine years, he has helped clients develop cost-effective strategies primarily by using the Internet to reach seniors and minorities.

A senior himself, Art has made presentations at local, national, and international association meetings and at conventions and trade shows. He has appeared on NBC several times and has been quoted as an authority on new developments in national publications and via the Web that affect seniors and retirees.

His latest venture, *www.RetiredBrains.com*, is a suite of sites designed to provide information to seniors and retirees on a wide variety of subjects as well as connecting them with employers that have openings appropriate for retirees. While researching content for his Web site, Art began compiling the information that became this book. Art lives in Chicago with his wife Normin and his two Westies, Spocker and Duncan (pictured above).

Art can be reached at
artkoff@yahoo.com
www.RetiredBrains.com
645 N. Michigan Ave. Suite 800
Chicago, IL 60611